Advance praise for Chanah's Voice

A beautiful example of how to wrestle with God, Torah, and one's self. Ner-David's story overflows with her knowledge of our past, awareness of our present and hope for our future, both as Jews and as human beings.

Rabbi Brad Hirschfield, author, *You Don't Have to Be Wrong for Me to Be Right*

This profound meditation on spiritual integrity, vulnerability, and holiness is a must-read for anyone who values Judaism. Haviva Ner-David has once again illuminated the way for us, enlivening ancient concepts and imbuing them with deep spiritual meaning.

Rabbi Danya Ruttenberg, author, *Surprised by God: How I Learned to Stop Worrying and Love Religion*

Haviva Ner-David is one of the most original thinkers on the Jewish scene today. In *Chanah's Voice* she takes what have sadly become stale rituals and re-envisions them anew. Ner-David's powerful stories of family, tradition and love will inspire readers to find deeper meaning in their Jewish lives.

Ari L. Goldman, author, *Living a Year of Kaddish: A Memoir*

Haviva Ner-David is among the leading "refusers" of our time— refusing to choose between traditional Jewish practice and feminism, refusing to be cowed by those who cannot comprehend a woman or- dained by an Orthodox rabbi.

Chanah's Voice marks a new and important phase in her defiance of expectation and boundary.

Here, the iconoclastic halakhic feminist turns to the most traditional of Jewish women's mitzvot, and finds not the bromides of hearth and home, but new challenges, new insights, and, at times, new theological innovations.

This is a deceptively simple book, which is to say, not simple at all. Read it and have your horizons expanded.

Jay Michaelson, author, *God vs. Gay? The Religious Case for Equality*

I have always admired Haviva. I loved her first book, yet *Chanah's Voice* is more remarkable. It is not only a unique contribution to the literature of feminism and Orthodoxy but also a significant work that better fits the categories of theology and social anthropology than autobiography. Perhaps this is how all theological works should be: written engagingly in the first person, making accessible to the reader the struggle of an individual or community trying to make sense of one's relationship with God.

She questions and questions, while swimming, partying, raising children, dealing with illness, learning, teaching and more. Haviva wrestles on her journey through life, interfacing every day events and ritual acts with classical assumptions about tradition, the psycho-social understandings of the Rabbis, the new roles for men and women, and her longing for the Divine spark within. Through her ruminations, her arguments with herself, her changes of mind, we see that new roles are not simply the taking on or putting down of this tradition or that behavior but rather a cosmic change in the universe as we have known it. We watch, as her newfound sense of freedom grows along with her sense of holiness in all things.

For those of us who have chosen to remain within the framework of Orthodoxy and accept its authority, this work offers intellectual challenges and should be read with an open heart.

Blu Greenberg, author, *On Women and Judaism: A View from Tradition*

Chanah's Voice

A rabbi wrestles with
gender, commandment,
and the women's rituals of
baking, bathing, and brightening

Haviva Ner-David

Ben Yehuda Press

Teaneck, New Jersey

Published by Ben Yehuda Press
122 Ayers Court #1B
Teaneck, NJ 07666

http://www.BenYehudaPress.com

Ben Yehuda Press books may be purchased for educational, business or sales promotional use. For information, please contact:
Special Markets, Ben Yehuda Press,
122 Ayers Court #1B, Teaneck, NJ 07666
markets@BenYehudaPress.com

ISBN13 978-1-934730-44-7

Library of Congress Cataloging-in-Publication Data

Ner-David, Haviva, 1969-
  Chanah's voice : a rabbi wrestles with gender, commandment, and the women's rituals of baking, bathing, and brightening / Haviva Ner-David.
  pages cm
Includes bibliographical references and index.
ISBN 978-1-934730-44-7 (alk. paper)
1. Jewish women--Religious life. 2. Hallah. 3. Purity, Ritual--Judaism 4. Candles and lights (Judaism) I. Title.
BM726.N47 2014
296.082--dc23
          2013045918

14 15 16 / 10 9 8 7 6 5 4 3 2 1   20140316

Contents

Dedication

To Jacob.

May we continue to raise each other up and light each other's fires so that we can together immerse, again and again, and emerge always hand in hand.

Preface

When God created the world—so teaches the 16th century kabbalist Isaac Luria—the Divine vessels could not contain the Divine Light. The vessels shattered and fell to the material world and were transformed into the four elements: earth, water, fire, and air. But pieces of the Divine Light, in the form of sparks, remained attached to the vessels. These sparks of Divine Light can now be found in all of God's creations, and it is our duty on earth to elevate these scattered sparks to holiness. The initial shattering was no mere accident; it was part of the Divine plan all along. For just as a seed cannot grow to its final form without decomposing, so too the world cannot reach its perfected form without going through a similar process of brokenness and growth.

In other words, it was always part of the Divine plan for the world to shatter into tiny shards. In this way, we human beings could become part of the process of piecing together an elevated, even higher, more holy, form. When God punished Eve and said that Adam would rule over her, this was part of that shattering. It is now our role as human beings in the material world to elevate the sparks of relationship to bring the world to its final perfected form—in which cooperation and partnership, rather than power, will be the driving force.

Now Chanah, she spoke in her heart; only her lips moved, but her voice could not be heard.
— I Samuel 1:13

There are three sins for which women die in childbirth: a lack of care with regard to nidah (menstrual separation), challah (the separation of the dough-offering), and the lighting of the [Shabbat] lamp.
— Mishnah, Tractate Shabbat, 2:6

Why was she given the mitzvah (commandment) of menstrual separation? Because she spilled the blood of the First Adam; therefore she was given the mitzvah of menstrual separation.

And why was she given the mitzvah to sacrifice the first portion of the dough? Because she spoiled the First Adam, who was the first portion of the world; therefore she was given the mitzvah to sacrifice the first portion of the dough.

And why was she given the mitzvah of lighting the Sabbath lamp? Because she extinguished the soul of the First Adam; therefore she was given the mitzvah of lighting the Sabbath lamp.
— Bereshit Rabah, parashah 17

Introduction: THE ELEMENTS

CHaNaH: Challah, Nidah, and Hadlakat Ha-ner

Bread is made from just flour, water, salt, and yeast, as the earth is made from just earth, water, fire, and air.
— sign at Nadav Desserts bakery in Ramat Yishai, Israel, adapted from Carol Field, *The Italian Baker.*

SINCE I BEGAN to consider myself a Jewish feminist, I have always been a member of a women's spiritual group. For many years it was a Rosh Chodesh group, where we met to celebrate the New Moon, which has traditionally been considered a women's holiday in Jewish practice.

How did Jewish women in past generations celebrate this women's holiday? The Talmud (which was written by men) tells us that women celebrated by taking the day off from household chores. So, for one day each month, women did not do laundry or cook or clean. The men tell us what affected them—the fact that their laundry was not done, their dinner not cooked. But what did these women do instead?

Perhaps they met in groups like the ones I have been a part of and created a women's spiritual culture of which we have no official record. Perhaps they baked bread or did some other creative activity together while chanting. Perhaps they invented rituals around menstruation, child birth, and menopause. Perhaps they lit candles and treated the day like a monthly Sabbath dedicated to being instead of constantly doing.

We have no way of knowing what they did on their Rosh Chodesh day because official Jewish records (written by men) do not tell us. Women then did not write down what they did. They were not a literate culture. Yet that does not mean they did not lead spiritual lives. It is my feeling that one of the goals of Rosh Chodesh groups around the world is to recreate that culture—or create it anew in the spirit of our fore mothers.

When I lived in New York I belonged to a Rosh Chodesh group. When I lived in Washington, D.C., I did too. Then, when I moved to Jerusalem, one of the first things I did was find a Rosh Chodesh group. And then my Jerusalem Rosh Chodesh group disbanded, after over ten years of meeting. Coincidentally, a few members left the country at the same time, a good reason to rethink our format and recharge our spiritual batteries. It felt like time for a change.

So a handful of us remaining women decided to form a group that would meet more often, twice a month, with a more focused purpose.

At the time, I was going through a transitional period in my own Jewish feminist outlook. As a Jewish feminist, I considered myself obligated in all of the mitzvot, the men's and women's mitzvot alike. But, like most Jewish feminists, I had spent considerable time exploring those Jewish rituals traditionally considered "men's" mitzvot. Those were the Jewish symbols and actions I had been educated to believe were most central to Jewish practice. And the fact that they were traditionally considered off limits to women made them all the more attractive. But as I grew into a more mature feminism, I knew that in order to embrace my Judaism fully and discover my Jewish soul, I had to take a much-overdue journey into the three "women's" mitzvot enumerated by the Mishnah: challah (religious laws around bread baking), nidah (menstruation rituals), and hadlakat ha-ner (sabbath candle lighting). These three are often referred to by their Hebrew acroymn, "CHaNaH."

This acronym seemed to me especially fitting for these mitzvot because the biblical Chanah was the mother of prayer. The Rabbis in the Talmud modeled the way we pray the Amida silent prayer after the way Chanah prayed for a son in Shilo: Her lips moved but no words came out. (The priest Eli was less impressed; he thought Chanah was drunk.) My journey through these three mitzvot was in many ways a search for Chanah's Voice and an attempt to end her silence. To me, freeing her voice is one of the steps that needs to be taken in order to fix our broken world.

I suggested that an exploration of these three mitzvot be the focus of our new group, and the other women liked the idea. We decided to explore these three commandments together. In a culture that values what society has constructed as "male" over what society has constructed as "female", we decided it was time to delve deeply into those modes of spiritual expression that have been devalued by society and that were traditionally practiced by our female ancestors. We wanted to see if we could rediscover the spiritual meaning that must be inherent in these ways of reaching the Divine—not as an apologetic towards reassigning these modes to women alone, but as a way of reintroducing them and all they represent into our lives as Jewish feminists—to reclaim these modes of ritual expression—and into Jewish society in general (for men and women alike).

So we began our project with challah. And that is where my story begins...

EARTH

CHALLAH: Baking

When you enter the land to which I am taking you and you eat of the bread of the land, you shall set some aside as a gift to the Lord: as the first yield of your baking, you shall set aside a loaf as a gift; you shall set it aside as a gift like a gift from the threshing floor. You shall make a gift to the Lord from the first of your baking throughout the ages.
— Numbers 15:18-21

Let me not be misunderstood. I do not discount the value of intellectual labour, but no amount of it is any compensation for bodily labour which every one of us is born to give for the common good of all. It may be, often is, infinitely superior to bodily labour, but it never is or can be a substitute for it, even as intellectual food, though far superior to the grains we eat, never can be a substitute for them. Indeed, without the products of the earth, those of the intellect would be an impossibility.
— Mahatma Gandhi, *Harijan*, 10/15/1925, ,p. 335

Every long journey begins with a single step, and the first step may be nothing more ambitious than learning to bake whole wheat bread.
— from "The Work at Hand," by Carol Flinders (in *The New Laurel's Kitchen*)

THE TORAH COMMANDS that from each batch of bread dough, a portion (generally, a handful) be set aside as an offering to God.

In ancient times, this offering was given to the priests; now, it is burnt in the oven, uneaten. The ritual is known as *hafrashat challah*, "separating the loaf" and colloquially referred to as "taking challah." This mitzvah provides an opportunity to remember God when baking bread.

Challah literally means loaf. In my vocabulary growing up in modern Orthodox Jewish America, challah referred to a specific variety of loaf, the braided loaf that we bought on Friday at the nearest kosher bakery. Like most of our neighbors, we did not eat home-baked Sabbath challot. Ironically, the ancient women's ritual of taking challah had become the domain of the male mashgiach who supervises the kashrut in these establishments. (So much for the view that the mitzvah of challah was to expiate Eve's sin!)

I can recall only one childhood friend whose family baked challot. They had a delicious recipe passed down from a German grandmother, and so all of us in the neighborhood considered it a treat to go to their house for Shabbat lunch.

When my husband Jacob and I moved to Washington, D.C., Jewish bakeries were hard to find, so we started baking our own challot for Shabbat. As vegetarians, who did not serve meat at our Shabbat meals, we baked delicious, rich, melt-in-the-mouth challah using milk and butter without worrying about the prohibition in the Torah against mixing meat and milk. Our friends considered it a treat to be invited over to our house for a Shabbat meal.

However, we did not perform the actual mitzvah of taking challah. The dough we prepared did not use the amount of flour halakhah requires as the minimum to perform the mitzvah (two kilograms, or around 10 cups). Two kilo of flour yields at least six medium-sized loaves of bread, too much for us newlyweds, even with friends over for a meal.

In any case, we were baking challot to have delicious bread for Shabbat meals, not to engage in a transformative holy act. It did not enter our minds to purposely use 10 cups of flour, take challah, and raise our baking to the spiritual level of mitzvah. I had come to question my exemption from mitzvot that had been traditionally reserved for men, such as wearing tallit and tefillin, but I did not question that my baking habits exempted me from taking challah.

"When you enter the land" is how the Torah begins the passage commanding the taking of challah. Sanctifying the domestic act of baking took place when the People of Israel reached the "Promised Land," after forty years of wandering in the desert.

But ironically, when Jacob and I (and our two young children[1]) entered the promised land, we left challah-baking behind. With so many kinds of challot available in our Jerusalem neighborhood, why bake our own?

We moved to Israel in 1996 for ideological reasons. We wanted to be part of building a Jewish country that would reflect our understanding of Jewish values: *Always remember how it felt to be slaves in Egypt and never forsake your covenant with your Creator.* Jacob and I were not naive. We knew Israel was far from perfect, but I imagined I was moving to an Israel that at least would soon be at peace with its Arab neighbors, opening up the opportunity for Israeli society to focus on other pressing issues like religious pluralism, sexism, civil rights, and other humanitarian issues. I was neither emotionally nor mentally prepared for what came instead: years of attacks and counter-attacks that fed the flames of hatred and undermined hopes for peace and mutual understanding.

As my years living in Israel passed, I came to ask myself: *Has the experiment of rebuilding a Jewish country on this ancient homeland failed? Are the sacrifices not worth the benefits? Is it time for the Jews to pack up and leave? Is it time for me to pack up and go home?*

---

[1] Jacob and I now have seven children. We had five children when I wrote this book, and we added two more to the mix between the time I completed this manuscript and the book was published.

In asking the question, I found my answer: *Israel was now our home.*
We had created a life in Israel for ourselves. Moreover, packing up our
kids and leaving would mean abandoning our Israeli brothers and sisters
who had nowhere else to go. We realized we had no choice but to face
our responsibility to remain and help do our best to try and create a better future.

☙ ☙ ☙

But along with my decision to remain in Israel came an unconscious
decision to spend more time at home. Surrounded by terror and fear,
many of us Jerusalemites retreated into our homes. With cafes and buses
blowing up around us, we were afraid to go out and did so only when
necessary—to work, school, synagogue, or meetings.

Moreover, living in constant fear that at any moment tragedy could
ensue gave me the desire to embrace what was good and rich and re-
warding in my life: my family. I came to focus on creating a warm and
embracing home life and atmosphere, to make our home a haven for the
family and a place where our value system could take hold.

If my children would consider our home a nurturing, safe space they
would want to spend time in, perhaps they would also have positive associations with the values they learned there. And if I could create a strong
and rich family life for my children, perhaps they would feel supported
to go out into the world with confidence to discover their God-given
life's missions and live out their own personal life's journeys.

I soon discovered, to my discomfort, that to create that kind of household atmosphere, I now sought practices I once disparaged as "women's
work." Now I came to appreciate the value of these domestic duties. Putting up fresh soup in the morning to simmer in the crock pot in winter
so it would be ready when the kids came home from school; making sure
there was plenty of fresh fruit to snack on; baking delicious whole wheat
zucchini muffins that filled the house with a warm, inviting aroma; using fresh vegetables instead of frozen. These things, I realized, could
only happen with the investment of time and love.

Yet a supportive, loving home can still be insulating at a time when there is so much work to be done in the world around us. Perhaps, I thought to myself, retreat could be part of the healing process—a step towards strengthening ourselves so that we could later reach out to one another as whole, dignified, balanced human beings with clear priorities and values.

Homemaking, I came to understand, can be considered *tikkun olam*—repairing the world—as long as it is not only women who are doing it. Not so long before, I saw cooking, washing dishes, and folding laundry as nothing more than housework. Now I came to understand that both "women's work" and "men's work," work in the private sphere and work in the public sphere, have the potential for increasing holiness.

Rabbi Yehuda Aryeh Leib Alter (1847-1905), the Hasidic thinker known as the Sefat Emet, considered the Bible's juxtaposition of the law of "taking challah" with the story of the Israelite spies who are sent to scout out the Land of Canaan. The spies, as the biblical story goes, return with a slanderous description of the Promised Land as a "land that devours its inhabitants"[2] and discourage the Israelites from entering. What is the connection between this story and the passage immediately following that commands the taking of challah?

Bread, explains the Sefat Emet, is the most basic of foods. It comes from the earth; representing our human need for physical sustenance, it is very much of "this world." Thus, when we give a gift of dough to God even before the loaves are formed, we are elevating our need for physical sustenance into a holy act. Confronted with the essence of the material world, we respond with spiritual elevation.

By contrast, the sin of the spies reflected a failure to cope with the actuality of the physical world. The Land did not live up to their ideal, so they slandered it. Because the spies refused to live in the reality of "the lower world," they could not elevate it through their piety. Instead, they lowered the reality even more by describing it in a most disparaging way and convincing the Israelites not to enter the Land. They brought the

---

[2] Numbers 13:32

people down with them.

The response to the sin of the spies, therefore, is to practice the taking of challah upon entering the Land of Israel, to elevate the reality of this world through spiritual acts. And to this day, Jews continue this practice.

This teaching of the Sefat Emet, that struggle for holiness takes place in our response to the oh-so-flawed real world, was a comfort to me as my horizons of tikkun olam broadened to include not only the political but the personal as well.

No matter how challenging or hopeless my work of making a home for my family in Israel often seemed, I resolved to remember the Sefat Emet's teaching that every holy act, no matter how seemingly insignificant in the larger scheme of things, is a step in the direction towards uplifting our often-depressing reality.

And having made this resolution, as a first step in renewed elevation in the face of despair, I decided to reinstate our custom of baking Sabbath challot. This time, however, I decided to do more than bake challot for our family. I decided to prepare enough dough so that I could fulfill the mitzvah of separating challah. It would be a symbolic reminder of our mission, undertaken week after week, in my imperfect home called Jerusalem.

🌾 🌾 🌾

My return to baking challah did not start in my home. A Rosh Chodesh women's group I belonged to disbanded, and a handful of us decided to form a new, smaller group in which we would explore the three "women's mitzvot"—challah, *nidah*, and *hadlakat ha-ner*. We called our group the CHaNaH group, using the traditional acronym for these three mitzvot, and thereby evoking the mother of both Samuel the prophet and prayer.

We began with challah, because we wanted something physical and tangible we could do together as a group. The first meeting we baked challot together and studied the rules of separating challah. We also practiced Breema, a type of body work originating in Kurdistan that feels like a cross between yoga and massage. Working in pairs, we kneaded each other like kneading the dough.

At our second meeting we talked about possible meanings of this mitzvah of challah. The discussion was rich and provided much material to explore in future meetings. And the challot came out better this time. We were becoming more skilled and were making spiritual headway.

The third meeting, however, was the turning point. One of the women, Ruth, who was close to completing her rabbinic studies, led us in a healing chant while we kneaded our dough. "*El na refah na lah*, God, please heal her!" These are the words of Moses when he pleads with God to heal his sister, Miriam, after she had been stricken for speaking harshly against him.[3] Each of us brought into the healing circle the name of a woman who was either emotionally or physically ill, and we meditated on these women's names while we recited a chant lasting 18 minutes—the amount of time it takes to make Passover matzah, and the numerical equivalent of the Hebrew for "life."

At some point in the chanting, we lost ourselves in the rhythm of the chant and the kneading and entered a trance-like state. We felt energy flowing through us and bringing healing into the world. We then joined hands and sang the words of Psalm 90:

"*Yihi noam Adonai Eloheinu aleinu, umaaseh yadeinu koninah aleinu, uma'aseh yadeinu konineiyhu.* May the favor of the Lord, our God, be upon us; let the work of our hands prosper, O prosper the work of our hands!"[4]

We prayed that God accept our kneading as sacred work. We then separated the challah and recited the blessing in unison. Our feeling of partnership was strong. One woman pointed out that this is probably how challah making had been done in the past, by groups of women. In the past, before professional bakeries and supermarkets, women baked bread every day for their families. And baking bread then was a longer process than it is today and was harder physically as well. It began with grinding the flour on a mill stone. Doing it together would have helped them pass the time, helped them physically move the mill stone with the

---

[3] Numbers 12:13
[4] Psalms 90:17

power of a group, and turned what could have been a solitary drudgery into a time to share and connect.

The experience of that morning had been powerful for us all. I intensely felt the healing energy and a strong connection to this ritual. Through our group effort, we had elevated this already holy act to an even higher plane. We had turned the act of baking and taking challah not only into a way of sanctifying the bread by giving back to God, but also of using the positive energy that flowed through us to constructively affect the world.

That is the essence of what we as a group were trying to do: actualize this mitzvah on all levels. Performing a Divine commandment to fulfill God's Will is the basic level. An additional level is the spiritual meaning of the act, which includes studying and delving into the mitzvah. Then there is also the cosmic power inherent in the act itself, especially since we were doing it in a group. There is power in numbers in Jewish tradition. Two witnesses are required to testify in a court of law or to sign personal status documents; three are required to publicly thank God for a meal; and a quorum of ten is required to recite certain especially holy prayers. In this particular group, we created our own energy and let Divine energy flow through us, affecting the world by coming together to perform this holy act. We decided that from then on we would chant while kneading and that we would take turns choosing and leading the chant.

At the following meeting, another woman led us in a chant about releasing people from sticky situations. One woman was working with rye flour, having discovered that she was allergic to wheat flour. Rye flour is especially sticky. And so, as we chanted, we watched her literally turn her sticky goop into a nice ball of dough, fit for baking.

Before my turn came to lead the chant, I considered which verse I wanted to use. That past Shabbat had been Tu Bishvat, Jewish Arbor Day, and in honor of that holiday, Jacob and I had taken the kids on a bike ride along the side of a mountain on Friday afternoon, the eve of the holiday. The views were magnificent. It had been raining for two weeks straight. The almond trees were in full bloom, covered with light pink blossoms. It was breathtaking. After that experience, I wanted to sing praise to God. So I chose the verse, "*Halleluya, hallelu et Adonai min ha'aretz*, Praise be God. Let us praise God from the earth."

The next time our group met, we stood around my friend's kitchen table kneading and chanting: "*Halleluyah, hallelu et Adonai min ha'aretz!*" Then, as each woman felt moved, she added a line about different aspects of the world that praise God by their very existence: the almond trees in full bloom after the rain; the full moon rising in the sky; the snow up on Mt. Hermon; the Sea of Galilee full after years of drought; yeast bubbling in a mixing bowl; women kneading dough and praising God. When we finished chanting and wound down into some silent kneading, I was on a high. I felt connected to the earth and to the miraculous everyday physical wonders that surround me. I felt such a heightened sensitivity to the physical world that the sensations could only be described as spiritual.

After cleaning the kitchen, we retreated to the living room. We sat down in a circle on our mats and suddenly the whole house began to shake. We heard a loud noise, like something heavy falling in the next room. We were all silent for a moment—in shock, or perhaps wonder or fear. Then one woman who had lived for many years in Los Angeles said: "That was an earthquake." We all looked at her in disbelief. "Believe me. I know an earthquake when I feel one," she said.

The thought crossed my mind: Could God have sent the earthquake in response to our efforts? Could this be a replay of the earth that swallowed up the biblical Korach who rebelled against Moses' authority, arguing that "we are all holy"? There was, after all, an anti-establishment feel to our work together. We were taking religious power into our own female hands—chanting, creating spiritual energy, empowering ourselves as women to reclaim and re-interpret these ancient rituals for our modern, feminist consciousness. But would God really seek to destroy us? We were, after all, simply a group of women getting together to bake challah!

I decided to hear the message of the earthquake differently. Yes, the earth shifted beneath us, but it did not swallow us, because our egalitarian impulse was not Korach's sin. Rabbi Mordechai Leiner (1801-1854), the Ishbitzer Rebbe, explained that Korach's claim that "we are all holy"

is indeed true—even prophetic. All people *are* created in the Image of
God. Korach's problem was that he wasn't truly egalitarian. He and his
followers were not sincerely calling for an end to hierarchy; they wanted
to rule in place of Moses.

Our group, on the other hand, had no desire to replace one hierarchy with another. Our goal was true egalitarianism. We were exploring
an area of Jewish ritual that had been disparaged and undervalued by
the patriarchy and therefore also neglected by feminists like us. But our
intention was not to prioritize the traditionally female rituals over the
traditionally male rituals. We sought to integrate them all, de-gender
them, and open them up to every human being alike. As women who
felt comfortable in the traditionally male religious sphere, we wanted
to become equally as comfortable in the traditionally female religious
sphere, and were hoping our male counterparts would follow suit. The
dominance of the male approach had brought us only so far. It was time
to integrate a fresh perspective into the picture. We had no intention of
replacing a patriarchy with a matriarchy, but rather replacing a hierarchy
with a true democracy, in which all voices are heard.

Since our challah group met only every other week, I decided to begin
baking challot with my children on the off weeks. That is how I found
myself standing around the kitchen table with my five children (three
born in the ten years since we had moved to Israel). Laid out before us
were the ingredients for a whole-wheat challah. This was our first attempt at baking home-made challah together. We would make enough
dough for us to perform the mitzvah of taking challah with the blessing,
so each child would have a loaf of his or her own to knead. But before
there was dough, there was discord. Who would pour which ingredients
into the bowl? Who would mix?

"Take turns," I insisted. "We can't bake challah if there's fighting."

Nachum, the baby, was playing on the floor. He was teething and had
been cranky all day. Now he started to cry. I wondered: Was this such
a good idea? Picking up Nachum on my hip, I told the kids: "You guys

will have to do all the work."

Handing them the responsibility transformed their attitudes. Suddenly, they became a team. The eldest, Michal, read from the recipe and helped Meira and Hallel measure and pour. Adin (the second to eldest) mixed. Once the dough was firm enough to knead, I divided it into four pieces and gave each child a clump to work with. Hallel, who was almost three years old, covered herself in flour and dough. The kids were having a wonderful time.

When I decided the dough had been kneaded sufficiently, I told them to give their dough to me. I collected it all into one big ball and pulled off a piece the size of a small egg. "Repeat after me," I instructed the kids. *"Baruch atah Adonai, Eloheinu melekh ha'olam, asher kiddushanu bimitzvotav vitzivanu lihafrish hallah min ha'isah,"* the traditional blessing for taking challah. "Praised are You, Lord our God, Sovereign of the Universe, Who commanded us to separate out a portion from the dough." I set the oven to broil and threw the small handful of dough into the oven by itself to burn. Once it was charred, I discarded it.

Then I set aside the big hunk of dough in its bowl to rise, and I sent the kids off to bathe.

After the kids had baths and dinner, I noticed that the dough had more than doubled in size. It was ready to punch down and shape. Michal and Adin decided to make break-away challot with fresh herbs kneaded into the dough. Meira (third in line) wanted to make challah rolls in the shape of snail shells. Hallel wanted to make a pita. Interestingly, no one wanted to make a braided challah. Secretly, I was proud of their nonconformist creativity. But I made a braided loaf with my portion so we'd have at least one traditional-looking challah. An hour later, when the challot had risen a bit more, I put them in the oven to bake.

The kids stayed up even later than usual so that they could see the results of our baking. By ten o'clock, at least Nachum was asleep in his crib. By eleven, the rest of the kids were in bed but too excited to sleep. The house smelled like a bakery. The aroma was one of fresh bread and rosemary. Jacob walked in, and, hearing the door shut, the kids jumped out of bed and pounced on him at once.

"Abba, we made challot! See! Aren't they beautiful! This one's mine!

This one's mine!" They all tried at once to show him their challot. The smell was just too tempting to wait. I chose one of the smaller rolls to divide into pieces and handed them out to everyone.

"Not bad," Jacob said. He smiled. I could tell he was impressed. "And healthy!"

I tasted my piece. It was sweet and grainy and totally delicious. The touch of baking the rosemary into the bread gave it that extra special tang to make it perhaps the best I had ever tasted.

This would not be the last time the kids and I would bake challot together. We would bake chocolate chip challot, challot shaped like animals, and challot with hard-boiled eggs baked inside. And I would manage to turn the activity into more of a routine so that the excitement didn't keep the kids up all night.

But although we grew more skilled and efficient over the months, our first challah-baking experience together remains magical. Each week now when we taste our challot, Michal says: "But nothing tastes as good as the ones we made that first time." And although we have tried to duplicate that recipe, we never have been able to get it to come out just the same.

🌾 🌾 🌾

After weeks of baking challot together, we noticed that our challot were not rising as well as they had at first. The process had lost some of its magic. We were not investing the process with as much fervor and holy intention. We had gotten lazy with our kneading. We were cutting corners. We needed help.

I soon realized that I needed Jacob back in my challah-baking life. When we made challot in Washington, D.C., it was a partnership. Although it was my decision to return to challah-baking, I started to resent having to do it alone with the kids. After all, Jacob also ate of the challot we baked each week. And so, one Thursday evening, when Jacob was home, I asked him to take over kneading the dough. The kids had become less enthusiastic and often lost interest in kneading before it was time to stop. I found I was not kneading the dough for as long as I should. Perhaps kneading could be Jacob's role in our family project.

Jacob turned out to be an excellent kneader—both in terms of the physical and spiritual results. In the kitchen he is slow, methodical and careful, whereas I am messy and fast and tend to work on three different dishes at once. He truly enters the task of kneading. It is clearly meditative for him, a spiritual practice. It calms him when he comes home tense after a particularly stressful day. And we all see and taste the difference in the challot.

🌾 🌾 🌾

Baking is much more daunting than other cooking. When baking, you must completely give yourself over to the recipe, put your handiwork in the oven, and then trust that it will come out right. Baking requires chemistry and precision, not to mention a strict adherence to the correct measurements, ingredients, and proportions. As your skills and intuition improve, you can experiment and improvise, but there is still something about baking that requires you to submit to the process. For me, this submission is challenging. Cooking, on the other hand, is by definition more creative. A cooking mistake might improve upon the original. Cooking recipes are like suggestions, but with baked goods, mistakes can be disastrous. Only a skilled baker can attempt to innovate.

My feminist soul asks: Could this be why baking was relegated to women? Perhaps this is one way that women are trained to be submissive and obedient, to follow orders and ask no questions. Maybe, by reclaiming the mitzvah of challah as a family, attended to by both male and female family members, we can turn this around.

Baking bread is miraculous. From grains we create something incredibly necessary and tremendously transformed, something more useful than what we started with, yet also something that does not lose its own essence in the transformation. So, too, when a baby is conceived. The sperm combines with the egg, becoming a home for a human soul, and is then "baked" for forty weeks in the womb. The genetic materials, the "ingredients," are necessary to create a human being. But the sum of the parts is so much more than either sperm and egg or flour and water!

"Women's work" need not only be about submission. It is a creative process that mirrors Divine Creation. Yet, this kind of creative energy is both bold and humble. It recognizes itself as part of a larger building process. It is about transforming what we are given into something better and recognizing that these kinds of daily miracles cannot occur by the hands of the baker alone.

I like the image of Jacob kneading dough. Submission to a process can be a good thing. Human beings can grow from practicing meditative, productive acts of submission like baking challah. This can be a healthy, broadening experience... as long as these acts of submission are not gendered, and as long as they are balanced with other creative, rebellious acts of taking control and initiating progress and growth.

🌾 🌾 🌾

During the first year I returned to challah baking, I was invited to teach at an annual conference in England called Limmud, a week-long Jewish study extravaganza, with sessions running from early morning into the night. If I taught five sessions, the organizers of the event would pay my way from Israel and give me free room, board and registration for the conference. Nachum was still nursing at the time, but the organizers said they could not guarantee I would be asked again the next year if I declined. So I accepted and took Nachum along.

Despite the freezing cold December weather, Limmud proved to be a memorable event. Seeing 3,000 Jews come together for a week to study Jewish texts and experience Jewish culture was worth schlepping a baby to another country. But since my return flight would not land until Friday, I assumed our family would forgo home-baked challah for that Shabbat. There was no way I was going to be able to swing that one!

But I was wrong. I hadn't anticipated how much our challah-making had entered our family life. When I walked in the door, the kids greeted me with: "Guess what! We baked challah with Abba last night!"

It's nice to feel needed. But it's even nicer to feel that what you do with and for your family, and the rituals you establish, are important to them. My goal as a parent is to nurture my children's unique personal

growth and development, not to create clones of myself—but it is grati-
fying when, every once in a while, the messages I send are received by
them and tenderly reproduced in their own behavior.

But most importantly, it's essential to have a partner who supports my
dreams and even shares some of those dreams, so that even when I am
not there to birth these dreams into reality, I can count on him to provide us with home-baked whole-wheat challot for our Sabbath table.

Whatever work in the home has now come to mean to me, I am
still not willing to sacrifice my work in the world. I have come to value
"women's work," but I also want to be involved in the work men have
traditionally done. I want to bake challah and wear tefillin. Or, more
accurately, I want both Jacob *and* myself to both bake challah *and* wear
tefillin. And that is not so simple. It requires juggling, sharing, organizing, and compromise. Sometimes frozen spinach will have to do when
we are both too busy all day to buy fresh; and sometimes the laundry will
have to sit unfolded for days. And sometimes a meeting will have to be
cancelled when a child is home sick; and sometimes the tefillin will have
to lie, untouched, in their bag, when other more pressing responsibilities
arise.

But the mental and emotional switch I made as the result of my journey into challah baking is that I now see all of these aspects of life as
spiritual. Baking challah requires not only faith and submission to a process, but also patience and an ability to be present in the moment—like
all nurturing, creative work.

When my oldest child, Michal, was born, my outer world changed
and so did my inner world. To suddenly have a newborn to care for was
a shock. Raising a child is a productive and grand endeavor, but day-to-
day care-giving activities are not particularly intellectually satisfying. I
would change a diaper only to have the baby decide that a clean diaper is
an even better place to poop than the dirty one. Or I would finish nursing the baby and before I knew it, the baby was hungry again.

Despite the challenges of this consuming experience, I loved being the mother of a newborn. I loved nursing. I loved dressing my new baby. At first I tried to read books while nursing, but as Michal grew older, reading while nursing became more difficult and unnecessary. Instead, I spent the time watching her, playing with her fingers, or letting my thoughts wander. Caring for an infant prepared me for parenting in general. As time went by, I learned to let go, to enjoy sitting in the park with my kids, making them dinner, even folding the laundry. I became less goal-oriented, less achievement-oriented, and learned to just be, to be present and alive in the moment, and for that to be enough.

Is this state of being the end goal that the positive time-bound mitzvot—like laying tefillin and reciting the Sh'ma—are meant to achieve? Is this why women, historically the primary childcare providers, are exempt from these mitzvot? Did they learn the art of being present in the moment from their nurturing work and daily household tasks? The Mishnah tells us that women are exempt from positive time-bound mitzvot, but it gives us no explanation as to why. Fourteenth-century Rabbi David ben Joseph Abudraham explains that women serve their husbands; if they are obligated to perform time-bound mitzvot, they will feel torn between serving their master ("*ba'al*," the Hebrew word for husband, also the word for master) and serving their Creator, and the result would be tension in the home. In the 13th century Rabbi Jacob Anatoly says that it is a woman's God-given role to serve her husband. Therefore, it made no sense to obligate her to mitzvot that would take her away from the job God meant for her to do.

Rabbi Samson Raphael Hirsch, writing in the 19th century, suggested that women are spiritually superior to men (both innately and due to their more cloistered existence away from the temptations and distractions of the world), and therefore do not need to perform all of the 613 mitzvot. Contemporary Rabbis Emanuel Rackman and Norman Lamm posit that women are more aware of the sanctity of time because of their monthly bodily cycles and therefore do not need the positive time-bound mitzvot, whose purpose is to make us aware of the sanctity and cyclical nature of time.

Another popular contemporary explanation for the exemption of women from positive time-bound mitzvot is that women's time must be flexible so they can devote it to raising children and homemaking, responsibilities as important as the mitzvot from which they are exempt. Rabbi Moshe Feinstein, the revered 20th century Ashkenazi authority on halakhah, assumed this explanation for women's exemption from positive time-bound mitzvot.[5]

I doubt these contemporary explanations capture the actual historical reasons for the exemption. Women in talmudic times did not live as cloistered an existence as did women in 19th century Europe. Moreover, as in 19th and 20th century Europe, if the couple was not wealthy, neither would have had the time to lay tefillin in the mornings; and if they were wealthy and had servants, both the man *and* woman would have had the time. In talmudic times, wealthy women hired wet nurses and servants for most of the homemaking and childrearing work.[6]

More likely, women were exempted from these mitzvot for reasons closer to those suggested by Rabbis Jacob Anatoly and David ben Joseph Abudraham back in the 13th and 14th centuries. Women's role in Jewish society was to be subservient to their husbands and enable the men to perform the important work, which included these most prestigious mitzvot. Another factor may have been the desire to keep these mitzvot in the hands of men to safeguard their sanctity and prestige. If women, second class citizens, began to perform these mitzvot, they would lose their value.

It seems from the Talmud itself that "positive time-bound mitzvot" was a descriptive category rather than a prescriptive one. In the discussion on the Mishnah's statement of the general principle that women are exempt from all positive time-bound mitzvot, the rabbis of the Talmud bring so many exceptions to the rule that they conclude that one cannot learn anything from general principles. Most probably, women did not commonly perform a number of mitzvot for the reasons stated above, and only later were these mitzvot lumped together and given a name so that women could be officially discouraged from performing them. This seems especially likely since there are so many mitzvot that are time

---

[5] See Rabbi Moshe Feinsteins's responsum on "Women's Liberation" in his book, *Igrot Moshe*, Orech Hayyim 4, siman 49.

[6] See Judith Hauptman's discussion of this topic in her book, *Rereading the Rabbis: A Woman's Voice*, on pages 226-227.

bound that women are not only obliged to perform but that are even considered special "women's mitzvot." Is any mitzvah more time bound than lighting Shabbat candles, for instance, or all of the intricate internal vaginal checks required surrounding the menstrual cycle?

This means that when women's exemption from the category of positive time-bound mitzvot was established, the issues were sociological, not spiritual. Women's exemption preserved men's power and kept women in their subservient role; it was not about women inhabiting a higher spiritual plane. The Talmud has too many derogatory statements about women for one to believe that the ancient rabbis considered women to be closer to God than they were. If the rabbis truly believed this, they would have let women make the rules! For the Talmud, the mitzvot are not a consolation prize. They are a privilege and an honor. They are humanity's side of the covenant with our Creator.

The historical truth, however, whatever it may be, does not detract from the power of our own experience of mitzvot. Could caring for my children stand in for formal ritual acts? Could taking the time to steam organic carrots and mash them rather than buy baby food in a jar substitute for laying tefillin? No. Men and women need both: the everyday activities of family life that root us in our present reality, as well as the more formal mitzvot that give us a tool box with which to create ritual around our life experiences and transitions, imbue our existence with meaning, and connect us to a line of ancestors who dealt with similar life experiences and transitions throughout the generations. With that grounding in our tradition, we will be empowered to reap from that ancient wisdom appropriately and leave aside what should remain in the past, thus making our unique contribution to the chain of progression in a way that feels continuous not disconnected.

Nevertheless, it may be that when we are caught up in nurturing, we do need these mitzvot less. Perhaps we can be easier on ourselves when we miss yet another morning of wrapping tefillin because we were searching for our son's shoes. Perhaps we can be more forgiving of ourselves when even on a more smooth morning, we, again, resort to a quick wrapping and unwrapping of the tefillin with only the most essential prayers thrown in. And maybe in the years when homemaking is at its most intense, we can even allow ourselves to take a break from some of the more formal mitzvot that take away from the time we need to spend with our children or spouses or in simply keeping afloat of household chores.

For instance, someone working a full-time job already has little enough time for family and communal life. How much time should he or she set aside for serious Torah study? Leaving home in the evening to study Torah makes sense if studying Torah is the highest Jewish value— and there are stories in the Talmud of scholars leaving home for years on end that would seem to support that position. But I would question Torah study that comes at the expense of other Jewish values including family, community involvement, and making the world a better place.

I have come to the conclusion that the rabbis exempted women from certain mitzvot to ensure that men are free to serve God through mitzvot, and that the mitzvot not lose their status and, therefore, their power to inspire awe. For the rabbis, the impact of this exemption on women's spirituality and ability to serve God was acceptable—if the question of women's spirituality was even considered.

Today, however, women are equal citizens in secular society (at least officially) and are not expected to sacrifice their self-fulfillment for men. Exempting women from mitzvot no longer makes sense. Even as I have come to value homemaking and other nurturing activities once considered more feminine (such as communal work), I am still not willing to consider them "women's work." To be full, balanced human beings we all need to be engaged in both the public and private spheres, in nurturing acts as well as acts of self-fulfillment. Men, therefore, should take challah and women should wrap tefillin, and vice versa. If we value both of these experiences, and if we see neither gender as subservient to the other, we should settle for nothing less.

The growing presence of same-sex couples in our communities, who have joined together to sanctify their relationships and build families together, highlights the absurdity of dividing roles along gender lines. Should the children of lesbian parents have no model for performing the mitzvah of tefillin? Should gay men not bake challah with their children? Should each member of the couple be assigned a traditional gender role?

How much more sensible to share these mitzvot so that no one member of the couple loses out spiritually and no mitzvot are neglected!

Nevertheless, we should not take the rabbis' concerns lightly.

Will the mitzvah of wrapping tefillin lose its sacred aura if women begin to practice it? Not if we reckon women to be just as important as men. And not if we remember to value homemaking as akin to other, more formal spiritual acts. We need to shatter the hierarchical model altogether, not replace the current hierarchy with another.

But what of the concern that the family unit will suffer if we step away from homemaking to perform time-bound mitzvot? Will we all—men and women alike—be able to make time to perform the positive time-bound mitzvot daily and simultaneously give homemaking the attention it deserves?

Perhaps not.

But I am not suggesting that women strive to be men with all that the category entails in the halakhic rabbinic system. Rather, if it is impractical to expect everyone to lay tefillin every day at every point in their lives, perhaps we need to rethink the nature of this obligation for everyone—men and women *alike*.

Taking this notion seriously means creating a new halakhic category. Rather than dividing Jews into two groups, men and women, one obligated in time-bound mitzvot and one exempt, we should simply call a Jew a "Jew." This new "Jew" will not be a member of a hierarchical, gendered Jewish society, and therefore, we need a new paradigm for how this new "Jew" should relate to mitzvot.

Perhaps the very notion of obligation is no longer the appropriate model for understanding mitzvot. In our day and age, religious practice stems more from personal choice than communal or even Divine obligation, and our understanding of what it means to be a mitzvah-observing Jew should reflect that. No longer are Jews born into a community which defines roles and sets religious expectations from which there is no escape. People choose to observe mitzvot when they could just as easily ignore them. They choose to be part of a community of Jewish religious practice when they could just as easily walk away from their Jewish identity and observance. The theology that assumes obligation comes only from God is therefore no longer relevant for most of us.

Instead of an obligation imposed from without, Jews practice mitzvot because of a commitment from within. One might even make a commitment to a specific religious community or approach, or even make a commitment to God, and by so doing obligate oneself to observe mitzvot—but the option to not make that commitment is equally real.

I propose, then, that we accept this sociological reality as a new theological paradigm of religious practice. Between the traditional positions of inescapable obligation and unrelieved exemption, the model of commitment represents a middle way, a paradigm that combines these two rabbinic models. This new commitment model evokes the seriousness of obligation but suggests that the obligation comes as a heartfelt gift, a *terumah*, from the individual Jew.

As a gift to the merciful God, the commitment to mitzvot has limits. Built into it is the flexibility that the earlier system achieved through exemption. I do not believe that God wants us to dedicate ourselves in a way that brings too much turmoil into our lives on earth and too much tension into our relationships and certainly not in a way that removes us from nurturing work. Changing the baby's diaper takes precedence over wearing tefillin, but the presence of a baby does not let one off the hook entirely from a commitment to performing this act in some way or degree.

Within this model of commitment, prioritizing and balancing our commitments and values remains an ongoing responsibility. This is more complicated than dividing roles based on gender, but I see this as the only option in an egalitarian, non-hierarchical society.

The traditional model assumed there was an enabler in the picture to maintain the household. Therefore, if we rid ourselves of hierarchy, we must redefine what it means to perform these mitzvot "properly." If we let go of the notion that mitzvot like tefillin must be performed every day and with total *kavanah*, full-hearted mindfulness, then performing them will not feel as impossible a task as it sometimes does when trying to balance this with other tasks of value. That way, one can commit to the mitzvah of tefillin without having to commit to its perfect performance. What becomes important is one's personal connection to and feeling of ownership over the ritual act of wrapping tefillin to the best of one's ability amidst personal limitations and constraints, while also remembering the inherent value of the work that is exemplified by the "women's mitzvot."

It is important to remember that even if we can't do the actual wrapping every morning, we are not missing out on the formal ritual experience completely. Childcare, cooking, and making a home, when done with the right state of mind, can put us into that same state of living beyond time and beyond ourselves that is part of the experience of serving God through the "positive time-bound commandments."

By the same token, if we are too exhausted on Friday to bake our own challot, we can forgo the mitzvah of taking challah once in a while. Thankfully, Judaism blesses us with more than one ritual way to offer ourselves up to God. What is essential is that we, the new "Jews," remain committed to both what are traditionally considered "men's" forms of spiritual expression and what are traditionally considered "women's" forms of spiritual expression as integral parts of our religious practice.

If the goal of feminism is indeed for women to be changed by men and for men to be changed by women, and for society as a whole to be changed as a result, then we have no choice but to open ourselves to becoming the "New Jews" with a totally new, untraditional, relationship to mitzvot.

And yes, this will mean Judaism as we know it will be somewhat transformed. But we should not fear this inevitability; this is all part of using the broken pieces of the world to build a better place for everyone in it.

🌾 🌾 🌾

After several months of weekly challah baking, I attended a workshop on baking sourdough challah. Making bread had become a part of my life and I wanted to expand my repertoire.

The workshop was led by Miriam, an amazingly energetic woman in canvas clogs and a flowing print cotton jumper, her hair wrapped up on her head in a gauzy burgundy cloth. Miriam explained sourdough, and then proceeded to bake, before our very eyes, delicious sourdough herb challot.

I noticed a garden of sprouts on the window sill and asked Miriam about them. She explained that six days of the week she eats a strict raw-foods diet and eats cooked food only on Shabbat. Miriam sprouts all her own grains in order to receive maximum nutrition from them. Choosing and preparing food is a hallmark of Miriam's identity. Everything in her kitchen was basic, healthy, wholesome and unprocessed.

This was a revelation for me. I had always been a healthy eater, preferring whole grains and lots of vegetables and fruits in my diet; and Jacob and I and all of the kids are vegetarians. But I was never particularly connected to the food I ate. I did not give much thought to where the food came from, and I never enjoyed preparing it. My ideal would have been healthy take-out around the corner from my house. But Miriam inspired me to think of food preparation as a spiritual process.

Reality set in when I returned home. I could never expend the amount of time and energy that Miriam did on food preparation. Nevertheless, her example embodied an ideal. Even if I fell short, Miriam would be my reminder to try to live a life more in tune with food, its source, its nutrition, and its preparation.

Now that I was baking challot each week, I did feel more of a kinship to Miriam than I ever could have before. I was beginning to experience the process of nourishing myself and my family as both routine *and* fulfilling. The idea of going out to buy impersonal challot felt stranger and stranger. My experience was beginning to feel like the reverse of the Sefat Emet's interpretation of the mitzvah of "taking challah." For the Sefat Emet, baking bread was a mundane act that required elevation. For me, baking bread had become the act that elevates the mundane.

I decided that I was ready to rise even higher. Sourdough bread was the next step in my bread making journey. I took Miriam's instructions from my bag and read:

The novel thing about sourdough baking is that it requires that you keep something alive in your fridge. Sourdough "starter" is a batter of flour and water, filled with living yeast and bacteria. The yeast and bacteria form a stable symbiotic relationship, and can live for centuries, a thriving colony of microorganisms. To make sourdough bread, you blend the starter with some flour and make dough. The yeast propagates, and leavens your bread.

As per her instructions, I mixed a cup of flour and a cup of warm water in a small glass bowl, covered it with a lid, and set it aside in the warmest place in the house, right beside the oven. That was all for today. Daily, for about a week, I would have to replenish it, which meant replacing half of the contents of the bowl with a half cup of water and a half cup of flour. After three to ten days, the starter would begin to bubble and smell like beer. Once this happened, I would keep it in the refrigerator, replenishing it once a week and pouring off or stirring back in the watery liquid that would form on the top of the starter.

It really was not as complicated or time-consuming as I imagined it would be.

🌾 🌾 🌾

The phone rang. It was one of my friends from my CHaNaH group. She wanted to try baking sourdough bread, but she had no starter. I was happy to oblige. I scooped out two cups of sourdough starter, put the sticky mixture into a Tupperware container, replenished my own starter, and began the walk to her house. As I strolled, I remembered a legend recorded in the Babylonian Talmud[7] about a priestly family, the House of Garmu, who knew how to bake the sacred bread of display used for worship in the Temple — but refused to share that secret. The Rabbis removed these priests from their positions and brought in bakers from Alexandria; but these bakers could not replicate the sacred bread. In the end, the Garmu family were returned to their post after insisting on double their former salary. When asked why they had refused to share their secret, they replied that their father had prophesied the destruction of the Temple and had told them not to share this secret of the baking of the bread of display, lest the secret fall into the wrong hands and be used for idol worship. The House of Garmu was then praised for its actions.

In the past, the Talmud's positive twist on this family's refusal to share their bread-making secret had bothered me. I tended to agree with

---

[7] BT Yoma 38a

the Mishnah's understanding of the story[8], which records this family's actions as disgraceful. I too saw the House of Garmu as ungenerous—even greedy. After all, they refused to bake for the Temple, an act of Divine service, unless their salaries were doubled! Though we are meant to understand their actions as foresighted, I saw them as the opposite. They may have prevented the bread of display from being used for idol worship, but wasn't it this kind of lack of sharing and partnership, this kind of lack of trust in others, the *"sinat chinam,"* unrestricted, arbitrary hatred, that, according to tradition, led to the destruction of the Temple in the first place?

This made me think once again of the story of the Israelite spies. The Sefat Emet faulted the spies for slandering the Land of Israel. But, upon a more careful read, we see that the spies actually praised the Land. They called it "a land flowing with milk and honey." It was the people living in the land that they feared. The fault of the spies was not a lack of faith in the Land itself, but rather a lack of faith in themselves, each other, and God. Like in challah-baking, faith and trust are as important as having the right recipe and technique. Moreover, without a community, performing the mitzvah of taking challah becomes quite difficult because of the sheer amount of dough required. The mitzvah becomes weighty rather than uplifting. My journey into challah was teaching me something about partnership and working together. I had become part of a bread-baking community.

As I handed some of my sourdough starter to my friend, I felt satisfied. Rather than hoard my "secret" like the House of Garmu, I was sharing it. This felt like a better way to bring redemption. Rather than worry about sacred secrets being used for profane purposes, we can share them and trust that our generosity of spirit and faith in humanity will seed a similarly generous and faithful spirit in others.

The Lubavitcher Rebbe, Rabbi Menachem Mendel Schneerson, explained the mitzvah of challah in a way that supports this holistic under-

---

[8] BT Yoma 3:12

standing of spiritual work:

At the basic level, taking challah sanctifies the bread we eat by giving from it a gift to God. It is the bread that is the essence of the ritual; as the verse says: "*Vihaya bi'achlechem milechem ha'aretz*, and it shall be when you eat from the *bread* of the earth" (Numbers 15:19).

The challah offering reminds us that "*Lo al ha'lechem levado yichyeh ha'adam.* Not by bread alone does man live" (Deuteronomy 8:3). We need both the material and the spiritual to live a full and balanced life. And even the most basic material things in life can be spiritual. By making an offering to God from the bread, we elevate the bread (our sustenance) and therefore ourselves.

Nevertheless, the challah is taken from the raw dough, not from the baked bread. (Only if we forget to separate from the dough do we take challah from the bread itself.) So what is the dough's significance? Why is it preferable to offer the initial dough rather than the finished, baked bread?

Because the dough, explained the Rebbe, symbolizes unity.

With the addition of water, all the bread's separate ingredients become one mass. It is this moment of unity that God desires and that we aspire to.

How are we to achieve this unity? How are we to become like flour in water? In Jewish thought, water symbolizes Torah, our spiritual work in this world. Like water in dough, the work we do to connect to something larger than ourselves unifies the world's disparate parts. Torah charges us to achieve unity with the earth and with nature, unity with the oneness of the Divine, unity with our own spiritual center, and unity with all other human beings—no matter their race, religion, or physical or intellectual abilities. It is this unity which God desires as a gift. It is not enough to reach this state of unity internally, or in our own home or community; we cannot stop until the whole world is in that state of spiritual unity. This is the lifelong project of tikkun olam.

Sourdough is continuity. Add it to dough and it initiates the fermentation process and causes the dough to rise. The reaction of fermentation continues within the sourdough as long as it is cared for.

This is the way it is with Torah, our sacred tradition of trying to figure out how to relate to the Divine throughout the generations. As long as we continue to fuel ourselves, others, and our children with Torah in a caring and exciting way, the Torah will continue from generation to generation. Revelation at Sinai is like that first fermentation reaction that begins the sourdough process. That first encounter with the Divine was all that was needed to start the process of Torah's interpretation and reinterpretation. Like the living sourdough that I passed on to my friend, Torah is a dynamic, ongoing, life-infused tradition, not a static corpus.

Torah is alive. It can catalyze an endless number of dynamic reactions in the soul of each and every human being who "kneads the dough." Engaging with Torah, like baking bread, is a slow process requiring patience and faith.

But unlike the yeast of sourdough, which comes from the air, the discussion we call Torah requires access and empowerment. Until recently, women have lacked this access, waiting like matzot for freedom and revelation in order to rise. Just as I was privileged to have access to Miriam's sourdough baking class and the time to prepare the starter and thus have it in my refrigerator to share with my friend, I've been blessed with the access to Torah study that I am able to pass on to my children.

By committing to both challah-taking and Torah study, by sharing this commitment with others, and by passing it on to *all* of my children, the boys *and* the girls, I hope to begin to make amends for the catastrophe of the Garden of Eden. Not for Eve's "sin" of causing Adam's mortality, but for the imbalance that was introduced into the world when God punished Eve by placing her under Adam's thumb. Like a sourdough starter, Eve's action initiated a process the world needed to achieve the perfected state we hope it will one day reach. And it is my belief that this "sourdough" was kneaded into God's plan all along.

As the months passed, my connection with the ChaNaH group and the ritual of baking and taking challah only grew stronger. I had found deep meaning in taking challah. I had been uplifted spiritually by this "woman's mitzvah." I had found refuge in this sphere in response to the shattered hopes of the world around me in Jerusalem.

Was tranquility amidst chaos too much to demand from a ritual, no matter how holy? Three days after a bus was blown up by a Palestinian suicide bomber only a few blocks away from my home, my CHaNaH group met to bake challot. The bombing had happened on Rosh Chodesh Adar, the first day of the month in which Purim, the Jewish carnival holiday, falls. Our chant for that session was so appropriate for what we were all feeling. "*Hafachtah mispidi limachol li*, Turn my mourning into dance for me," from Psalms 30:12. It was a request of God to help us rise out of our abyss of sorrow and hopelessness.

In fact, the month of Adar brings this challenge every year. The Talmud[9] teaches that "*Mishenichnas Adar marbim besimchah*," that with the start of the month of Adar our joy increases. Yet I have come to expect something horrible to happen in Israel every year when Adar and the holiday of Purim come around. One year Baruch Goldstein massacred a group of Muslims praying in The Cave of the Patriarchs in Hebron; another year Jewish Israeli children dressed in their Purim costumes were killed in a terrorist attack; another year we were walking around with gas masks instead of Purim masks, waiting for a war to start. This year's suicide bombing down the street from my house seemed to fit a pattern.

Bad things happen all of the time, to all types of people, no matter what month of the year. Yet it seems—whether statistically true or not—that they happen more often to the Jewish People around the time of Adar. The Purim story itself is an example. That story ended well for the Jews, but imagine what it was like to live in Persia when the royal decree to kill all of the Jews was announced! In the end, the Jews were saved by Esther's and Mordechai's political maneuverings, but the impending disaster was frightening enough. It reminds us of the unfathomable horrors that did come to pass less than a century ago, the Holocaust.

Moreover, as in Israel today, the intended massacre of the Jews lead to

---

[9] BT Taanit 29a

a Jewish massacre of the Persians—a historical cycle that was physically tragic for the Persians in the short run but morally tragic for the Jews in the long run.

Traditionally, the Talmud's statement about Adar joy is understood not as a description, but a prescription. We are not promised that Adar will always turn out to be a happy month, but rather we are instructed to *make* it joyful. Perhaps this is exactly why we are told to be happy in Adar of all months: because it is so difficult! The message of Adar is to find joy in the face of sorrow and tragedy, even horror. It is easy to be happy when the world looks bright, but the challenge is to find a glimmer of hope, focus on it, and build it up so that it transforms your outlook. And this is a lesson to be applied to every month of every year.

Purim itself is the holiday of turning things on their head: Haman is hanged on the gallows he prepared for Mordechai, the murderers are murdered, and the mourning of the Jews is turned into celebration. In the megillah, the Scroll of Esther which is read twice on this one-day holiday, we read that the fate of the Jews was turned upside down: "*Vi-nahafoch hu.*"[10] And so, it was fitting to ask God to raise us up out of our depressed state after the suicide bombing.

The woman leading the chant had come with words but no tune. She said she wanted us to together create a niggun, a melody. One woman started to hum until she came up with the first part. Another woman jumped in with a second part, and we all joined in. The melody reminded me of a traditional Hassidic niggun, and as we lost ourselves in the mood, I felt akin to my Eastern European Jewish ancestors in the shtetl, singing niggunim like this one in the face of pogroms, persecution, and poverty. I closed my eyes and felt the presence of these ancestors. I felt them joining in our song. We six women in 21st century Jerusalem had created a Hassidic niggun! One woman began drumming on the table. Another began swaying. I threw my dough in the air, and another said: "Whoopee!" We were laughing and singing and even dancing. Through the mitzvah of challah, our mourning had turned to dancing.

---

[10] Esther 9:1

A month after Purim comes Passover. Bread is forbidden on this holiday, and flour that has been touched by water must be discarded. I had
kept my sourdough starter alive since November, and now, five months
later, I would have to simply throw it out. It was difficult to discard
something I had invested in, something that I valued. But then again, it
would also be nice to start afresh. While it is so satisfying to hold on to
something, it is also satisfying to learn to let go.

When I was a child, I watched my mother turn our suburban New
York home upside down during her zealous Passover cleaning. She
searched each room for forbidden leaven, chametz, and for the dirt and
junk that had piled up since the last Passover. The cleaning had to be
finished a few days before Passover, in order to cook for the two huge
seders, the holiday meals.

Later, as a young teenage feminist, I resented the fact that my mother
(with the help of our house cleaner) did all the cleaning and cooking
before the seders, while my father led the ritual aspect of these meals.
I saw my mother as enslaved to an exaggerated notion of the halakhic
requirement to rid one's home of chametz, which I thought was totally
antithetical to the notion of Passover as a holiday of freedom. I told
myself that I would never be subject to this inequity. I would clean the
minimum amount required by Jewish law and spend the rest of my pre-
Passover preparation time studying to be able to contribute to the content
of the seder. I would stress the intellectual and spiritual side of Passover
preparation rather than the mundane, physical side.

However, as I grew as a religious feminist, married, had children, and
set up a Jewish home in Jerusalem, I realized that *someone* had to clean.
Even if Jacob and I shared this work, I still had to focus much of my pre-
Passover preparation energy on cleaning. The truth is, even if a search
for chametz does not truly require turning one's entire home upside
down—with small children it practically does! The chances of finding
a half-eaten cracker almost anywhere in the house are pretty high with
a toddler walking around. And while a dusty cracker under the coach is
not problematic according to the letter of the law because it is not really
edible, once we were already cleaning in a labor-intensive way, Jacob and
I figured we might as well do a real spring cleaning. This, I imagine, is

how my mother, grandmother, and great grandmother felt as well.

I had another reason to embrace Passover cleaning. When I began serious study of feminist theory, I learned that in a society with a gendered division of labor there is often greater value placed on the work done by those of a higher social status. In a gender-stratified society, what men do is valued more highly than what women do simply because men do it—even when their activities are similar or the same.

This analysis suggested that the issue of Passover cleaning was not as simple as I had thought. I had devalued house work simply because it was women who were doing it. Of course this was tied in with the fact that they were overlooked as possible leaders of the seder. It's not as if women have chosen cleaning from among all the other options of religious expression within the traditional framework. Nevertheless, I underestimated the halakhic and spiritual significance of the work that my mother, her mother, and her mother's mother had been doing for generations of Passovers. Ironically, my feminism had led me to disparage my own mother and the labor of her hands. The thought was sobering. Perhaps if the men had been cleaning the house for Passover all along I might have considered *that* the essence of the Passover experience.

This realization helped me to understand that all mitzvot are important: taking challah and wrapping tefillin, cleaning for Passover and leading the seder. Women may involve themselves further in practices not traditionally considered their own without abandoning the customs of their mothers. So, too, for men. When men become more involved in the spheres of Jewish life they have not traditionally engaged, like cleaning for Passover, they need not abandon the customs of their fathers. But, of course, this requires true partnership and compromise if it is going to work.

So there I was, undertaking a thorough spring cleaning before Passover, much as my mother had done before me. And much to my surprise, I did not find it as burdensome as I had imagined it would be. In fact, I found it spiritually powerful—even transforming. As I sorted, wiped, and scoured, I felt a cleansing taking place within me. Although I was engaged in an activity that I had seen as an expression of women's servitude, I felt myself psychologically and spiritually liberated, like the freed

Jewish slaves. And right beside me, Jacob was working as hard as I was to clean the house for Passover—thank God.

I turned to the Zohar, a mystical commentary on the Bible that is the central text of Kabbalah. There I found much material to validate my experience. Commenting on the Torah portion of Titzaveh, the Zohar associates chametz with the evil inclination and idolatry: "And such is the evil inclination like yeast in dough, because it enters into the insides of a person, slowly, slowly, and then it multiplies and grows more and more until all of the body becomes enmeshed in it. And that is idol worship, which is likened to the evil inclination." As we rid our homes of chametz, we are ridding ourselves of the evil inclination, of all the drives, all of our personal weaknesses, that are preventing us from being who we strive to be.

I find my Passover cleaning spiritually fulfilling, but I also engage in the other positive commandments associated with Passover. Jacob and I facilitate a seder each year, together. And each year, as I clean, I compile a list of all my own personal spiritual and psychological chametz—the foibles that prevent me from being what I would like to or could be. Then, when I burn the chametz on the eve of the holiday, I toss that list into the fire and watch it burn. This is a way, for me, of making sure that I don't lose perspective on the broader meaning of the holiday.

🌾 🌾 🌾

"Baruch Atah Adonai Aloheinu Melech Ha'olam, Hamotzi lechem min ha'aretz. Praised are You, Lord our God, Sovereign of the Universe, Who brings forth bread from the earth."

This is the blessing we recite before eating bread. Consider what a strange blessing it is! Does God truly bring forth bread from the earth? God brings forth wheat from the earth, but not bread. For wheat to become bread it must be harvested, ground, mixed with water, kneaded and baked—numerous acts, all performed by people, not God. The only time that God brought forth bread directly was when we woke each morning in the desert on the way to Canaan to find manna, food from the heavens, spread across the ground like dew. But if bread, unlike the manna, requires the intervention of human beings to come into being, why do we thank God for bringing "bread from the earth"?

A teaching from Rabbi Yitzchak Hutner (1906-1980) finally gave me insight into this question. In his book, *Pachad Yitzhak*, Rabbi Hutner explores the connection between manna and challah, the Sabbath loaves, in his discussion on the verses from Exodus 16:4-5 in which God tells Moses to instruct the Israelites not to collect manna on the Sabbath:

And the Lord said to Moses, "I will rain down bread for you from the sky, and the people shall go out and gather each day that day's portion—that I may thus test them, to see whether they will follow My instructions or not. But on the sixth day, when they apportion what they have brought in, it shall prove to be double the amount they gather each day."

Each Friday in the desert, God sent the Israelites a double portion of manna so that they would have enough for Shabbat, when the manna did not fall. We remember this miracle each Shabbat by placing two loaves of bread on the table to symbolize the double portion of manna.

Rabbi Hutner asks whether challah is truly a good stand-in for manna. Bread is the result of our daily toil in this world. Adam was cursed with having to work the soil to bring forth bread after he and Eve ate from the Tree of Knowledge. By contrast, the Torah calls manna bread from the sky. In the desert, the Israelites got a taste of what it was like in the Garden of Eden. When the Israelites left the desert, however, they returned to baking their own bread. Bread represents the opposite of their charmed desert existence under God's protective cloud.

The significance of challah, says Rabbi Hutner, is that it is not ordinary bread. Challah is the bread we eat on Shabbat, and Shabbat is called *"me'en Olam Habah,"* a taste of what it will be like in the World to Come. Therefore, all of the food we eat on Shabbat tastes a little better. So when we eat challah, we taste the World to Come. It is bread of this world and of the next. Manna was a gift from heaven, but it was eaten by human beings in this world. It too is of both worlds, really. And somewhere in between these two worlds is where challah and manna meet.

With this teaching of Rabbi Hutner in mind, I now understand the blessing over bread. When we were in the desert, God gave us manna. Having been reborn out of slavery, we were totally dependent on God. We were like suckling newborns, receiving sustenance directly from our mother. But God weaned us from the manna. When we entered the Land, we were told that we would have to make our own bread. Nevertheless, God did not want us to forget that without God, there would be no bread.

It is especially for bread, so emblematic of the partnership between human beings and God, and which, with its magical fermenting and rising action, could give us a false sense of power, that we need this blessing—lest we begin to think that it is by our hands alone that bread comes to be in this world.

This understanding of the blessing over bread helped me see the missing piece in the project of tikkun olam. Yes, we can strengthen our homes and families. And yes, we can even reach out to others. But the real healing can only happen when we connect to God, the Source of Life. Connecting to the Source means retaining constant faith in the Divine plan. It means refraining from slandering the world and instead working in partnership with the Creator to make the world a better place.

Connecting to the Source also means connecting to and protecting the land itself. If we destroy the very soil from which our food comes, there will be no chance of a perfected world, of a better future for us. There will be no Earth upon which to live.

As I sought new ways of connecting to the land, God answered my call: A couple planning an organic farm not far from Jerusalem needed start-up funds. They wanted people to join the farm by purchasing in advance one year's worth of weekly shipments of fresh produce. The husband had studied agriculture and wanted to experiment with some innovative ideas about organic farming. His wife would run the business aspect. The farm was named "Alei Chubeza," meaning "mallow leaves." Mallow is a plant that grows wild in Jerusalem and was eaten as a vegetable of last resort during various sieges of the city.

I signed up immediately. Not only would I meet my own needs and the needs of my family, but I could help a young couple make a living while fulfilling an ideological dream. It would be a few months before we would receive produce from the farm, the weekly shipment was never quite enough to feed my family of seven, and the farmers only sent what grew that week. So I also placed a standing order from a health food store in the neighborhood. Twice weekly they delivered organic fruits and vegetables and anything else in the store: goat milk, soy milk, whole wheat flour, organic beans and legumes, organic honey and oils, free range eggs—all with less packaging and therefore less waste. They even sold environment-friendly household cleaning supplies. I saw this as an investment in our health and future, as well as a way of voting with our wallets. It felt good to provide my family with healthy foods while protecting our planet. When I looked at this as a kind of kashrut ("eco-kashrut")—a Divinely-ordained, ideologically-based eating lifestyle choice—it became easier to spend the extra money.

One evening, a few months after I entered into our partnership with Alei Chubeza, a man with long dreadlocks and a crocheted bowl-shaped *kippah* atop his head knocked on our door. In his arms he held a large plastic crate overflowing with fresh vegetables. I noticed the dirt between his fingernails when I took the crate from him. When he left, I dove into the contents of the crate, which, I was told, would be picked up at the next week's delivery. The smell of tomato vines filled my nostrils as I sifted through this treasure trove. The carrots, with soil still on them, were attached to their leaves. I washed some and handed them out to the kids, who were sitting at the table eating dinner.

"Mmmm, these are delicious!" Adin said.

"They taste so different," added Meira.

"Like how carrots are supposed to taste," explained Michal.

Perhaps the most challenging and enjoyable thing about ordering from the farm is that I never know what I am going to get. Sometimes I don't even recognize what I am sent and have to look up how to prepare it. I have learned about different foods that I and my family may enjoy, rather than falling into familiar eating patterns. We also find ourselves eating what is in season—another way of getting ourselves more in tune with the earth.

These weekly deliveries connect me to the earth and to the source of our food. Having to clean the dirt off the potatoes is a benefit of being a part of this project. In at least this small way, I can narrow the gap between myself and the source of my food.

As members of this cooperative farm project, we look forward to the twice-yearly Friday afternoon visits to the farm itself. Sure, it's muddy and dirty and we have to throw the kids into the bath when we get home. But we would do that anyway on a Friday right before Shabbat. Visiting the farm, picking vegetables, and eating them on the spot is a special treat. The kids are thrilled to pick corn and eat it raw like candy, to dig a carrot or potato out of the ground, to see how soy beans actually grow.

We are pilgrims from Jerusalem to the farmland of Israel, reversing the ancient practice of farmers ascending to Jerusalem three times a year.

🌾 🌾 🌾

A month after Passover, Adin asked if we could bake challot. "We haven't in a long time," he said, and he was right. We had not baked challot since before Passover. How easy it is to let go of something; even if it is important ideologically, if it slips out of your regular routine, it's gone.

So I took out the whole wheat flour and the yeast (I had not yet mixed a new batch of sourdough starter since Passover), and by seven o'clock Thursday evening, our hands were deep into the sticky dough. By then, I didn't even follow a recipe any more. I mixed the yeast with the water and raw sugar, waited for it to bubble, added oil, honey, eggs, and salt. And to that, I added as much flour in varying proportions as seemed fit.

I made sure to use at least two kilo of flour, so we could "take challah" with the blessing. Otherwise, it would have been just baking bread. The sanctifying part—an integral part of the challah-making process for me at this point—would have been missing. So even if that seemed like a lot of challah, I didn't worry.

Two hours later, we were kneading and shaping. Everyone wanted to make braids this time, so I decided to form a few snail-shaped rolls with my dough. I rolled some rosemary and zatar into mine as well, for variety. Adin put rosemary on the top of his, and Meira stuck with sesame seeds. Hallel used zatar. Nachum was asleep, exhausted by the kneading.

Michal, an eleven-year-old-going-on-sixteen, was in her room on the computer, "Instant Messenger-ing" with her friends. She said she would pass when I asked if she wanted me to save her some dough to shape. This seemed to be a theme with her lately; she wanted to be more with her friends and less with us. It saddened me that she didn't want to join in the fun. However, I knew this was natural and even healthy at her age. And, as far as I knew, she continued to be totally open with us. So if she needed her space, I let her have it. She agreed to be available to help me later, watching the other kids and the challot while Jacob and I were out at a friend's fiftieth birthday party.

By 9 p.m., Jacob and I were out the door. The challot were rising on the kitchen table, Nachum was asleep in his crib, and the four older kids were watching a DVD. I told Michal that she should put two challot in the oven in an hour.

At 10 p.m., I called Michal to remind her to put in the first batch of challot. My friend, who was next to me when I called, asked if I bake challot every week.

"We go back and forth. It seems to come in waves with us," I answered.

"Well, I am impressed. I'd love to taste your challot."

"I don't know how they'll turn out. Each time they taste different. But I certainly made more than enough. Why don't you come over tomorrow morning to get one?" I told her.

Then I understood that there was no reason to worry about too much challah. People are always happy to eat home-baked bread. *I could make a custom of this*, I told myself. *Always make enough to pass around. In fact, perhaps this could be a modern way of "taking challah." In addition to setting aside a piece for God, I could always make sure to give away at least one loaf to a friend. This could be another way to elevate the bread: by sharing it with others.*

The next morning, Hallel woke me up. Her eyes were filled with tears.

"I wanted to put my challot in the oven," she cried. "Why did you do it without me?"

"You fell asleep, but do you want to see what yours look like?" I asked her.

"Yes," she sniffled. Then her olive-green eyes lit up at the sight of her creation. "You'll eat them tonight," I told her. "Now let's get you ready to go."

After the children departed to their schools, I put up a split pea soup to simmer all day in the crock pot to be ready just in time for Shabbat dinner. It's one of our ritual Shabbat soups. The doorbell rang. It was my friend's husband. He came to pick up a challah.

"With herbs or without?" I asked him.

"With, please," he said.

"Let me know what you think," I said. "Shabbat Shalom."

Yes, I think I will make a custom of this, I said to myself. *It feels right. Sharing gives others the chance to feel what it's like to have Shabbat bread rain down from heaven.*

🌾 🌾 🌾

Bread-baking has transformed me. Now that I make my own bread, at least most of the time, I feel closer to the Earth, to God, to my own inner voice, and to the voices of my women ancestors. I feel uplifted by the potential cosmic power that is set free in the world when I engage in this mitzvah, especially within a community of bread-bakers.

For a while I was a person who baked bread, but then I stopped, because that is all it was to me: baking bread. When I returned to bread baking, I realized that it was about "taking challah." It was about looking at bread-baking as a holy act.

Bread-baking is not just about the end result, that wonderfully tasty bread. There is something in the act of mixing the ingredients, kneading the dough, shaping the bread, watching it rise, and, of course, separating the challah and burning it in the oven, that, like any mitzvah, feels transforming. The dough and the baker are both changed in the process.

When I bake challah, I try to do so with the right *kavanot*, holy intentions—with a sense of connection to others, to the Earth, and to the Source of Life. In fact, baking challah (and, in fact, any kind of food preparation) has become like a prayer for me. It is a meditative prayer that enhances my connection to the Source of Life, and more importantly, I believe, a prayer that has the potential to effect cosmic change.

I think back to that day with my challah baking group, when our collective kneading and baking and chanting was so in tune with the cosmic force that we felt the Earth move beneath us. This mitzvah, I now realize, has the power to not only connect us to the Earth and her Creator, but to be part of the cosmic shifting of earth! The mitzvah of challah is about recognizing brokenness and building without ever destroying. It is about working with what we have and raising it to a higher level. It is also about opening ourselves to hearing all voices, not only those who dominated our understanding of Torah for so many years. It is about valuing *all* the work that needs to be done to better the world and encouraging everyone to do it, irrespective of gender. While men made the rules surrounding "challah-taking," it was mostly women who performed this sacred act. And so, when I, a female rabbinical student in the 21st century, perform this mitzvah, I am harmonizing a cacophony.

Experiencing bread making as a holy act has taught me the satisfaction of living a balanced life. My priorities have shifted. Now that I have discovered the power of baking and taking challah, I do not want to give this up in order to serve my community almost 24/7 as a conventional rabbi would most likely do. Similarly, I would not want to give up laying tefillin in order to serve my husband. The mitzvah of challah has challenged me to find ways to both wear tefillin and take challah, a symbol of keeping my life in balance.

If I become a rabbi who lays tefillin but abandons challah, I will have succeeded in gaining some measure of equality, but I will have done nothing to transform the society which created the inequality in the first place. Even worse, I will have reinforced the hierarchical values of those in power. It is way past time to challenge the assumption of inequality and to work toward balance.

With minds open to valuing all work and ears open to hearing all voices, the traditional assignment of roles along gender lines no longer makes sense. The configuration of the roles we assume in making and maintaining home and society will change when we all—men and women alike—participate in creating them together. These changes will arise out of love, desire, commitment, and passion rather than obligation and oppression.

It may turn out that this new model is not as orderly and efficient as the old one, but it can work because the new model will certainly be more just, more healthy, more balanced, and therefore more sustainable. It will leave room for individuality and creative expression. And if it makes possible the vision of a better world in which all voices—including Chanah's, and all women's voices past, present and future—are heard, then it will be more holy. It will ultimately bring us closer to what I believe God had in mind for us humans inhabiting the Earth.

Perhaps a message of total equality, a new paradigm of balance, commitment, cooperation, and sharing could not work in Korach's time. Perhaps his rebellion was as premature as it was self-serving. Today, however, we live in a democratic world, which has seen the rise of movements fighting for the rights of women, people of color, gays, people with special needs, and we *are* ready to receive this message. Each individual *is* holy and contains a spark of the Divine to be cherished.

WATER

NIDAH: Bathing

Do not come near a woman during her period of
menstrual ritual impurity to uncover her nakedness.
— Leviticus 18:19

Everything had changed suddenly—the tone, the moral cli-
mate; you didn't know what to think, whom to listen to. As if
all your life you had been led by the hand like a small child and
suddenly you were on your own, you had to learn to walk by
yourself. There was no one around, neither family nor people
whose judgment you respected. At such a time you felt the need
of committing yourself to something absolute—life or truth or
beauty—of being ruled by it in place of the man-made rules
that had been discarded. You needed to surrender to some such
ultimate purpose more fully, more unreservedly than you had
ever done in the old familiar, peaceful days, in the old life that
was now abolished and gone for good.
— Boris Pasternak, *Doctor Zhivago*

Poke the mikveh with the sticks of rational inquiry, and you
will find little there, other than the bruises inflicted by criti-
cism. As with love and desire, there is little reasonable about the
sacred. But enter the waters with a broken heart, and you may
find a wordless healing.
— Jay Michaelson, *God in Your Body*

WHEN I WAS A CHILD, I noticed that my mother would leave home one
evening a month and return with her hair wet. It was curious, because
she did not leave with a swimming pool bag. It was also mysterious because she would leave and return without a word—unlike her behavior
following other outings to the theater, a party, or a class.

The mystery of these outings continued until my junior high offered
a mini course on "Jewish womanhood." Taught by my synagogue's reb-
betzin (the rabbi's wife), the class was a combination of Jewish home eco-
nomics and sex education. One topic was "*taharat hamishpacha*," which
means "family purity," a euphemism for the rabbinic Jewish laws that
ban sex around a woman's menstrual period.

As we girls learned, from the moment a woman feels her flow or sees
signs of blood, she becomes ritually impure (*teme'ah*). Sex is taboo for her
at that time. After her period, she must count seven more "clean" days,
checking to ascertain that her flow has truly stopped. Immersion in the
waters of the mikveh (ritual bath) transitions her into the status of ritually pure (*tehorah*). Sex once again becomes permissible.

This immersion traditionally takes place at night. (There are a variety
of reasons for that practice.[1]) I finally understood where my mother went,
why she wouldn't tell us where she was going, and why she came back

---

[1] It is assumed that the couple will be having sex soon after she immerses, and since
some halakhic authorities do not encourage sex during the day, many mikvehs are open
for these women's immersions only at night (although they are open for men during
the day). In addition, some women might be embarrassed to be seen walking out of the
mikveh because of its sexual connotations.

The Talmud gives a more technical reason: It fears that if a woman immerses in the
daytime, her daughter—whom it is assumed is with her mother during the day helping
with household chores, as was the practice in that period—will be confused and think
that she is immersing the morning before her seventh "clean" day concludes at nightfall,
rather than the morning after.

At the mikveh I now run at Kibbutz Hannaton, all immersions for whatever purpose
are done individually and privately by appointment at the convenience of the client, irrespective of the client's gender or the time of day.

with her hair wet.

I don't remember how detailed the lessons were, because this all seemed rather strange and inapplicable to my adolescent life.

When the subject was reintroduced a decade later, it had more personal significance. I was engaged to be married, and, coincidentally, the officiating rabbi was the husband of this same woman who had taught the "Jewish womanhood" course years before. When we met to discuss our ceremony, the rabbi asked if I'd like to have a session with his wife about the laws of "family purity" and mikveh.

Back in junior high school, her class came too early; by the time I was engaged, it was too late. I had grown into my identity as a religious Jewish feminist and had done my own reading. I found myself ambivalent about the practice of *taharat hamishpacha*. I knew the laws well and was leery of them. They resonated with misogyny, sexual repression, and blood taboo. Yet I had also read religious Jewish feminists I admired who spoke of ritual immersion as a spiritual feminist experience.

So I told the rabbi that I would study on my own. I needed to create an intimate relationship with this mitzvah. It was a relationship that would only become more complex with time, maturity, and deeper study.

When Jacob and I married, we decided to adhere to these laws on our own terms. The rules regarding *taharat hamishpacha* are complex, and as I studied them I came to understand that some of the practices had changed since the time of their origin. I accepted the main contours of the mitzvah: We abstained from sex for a given period each month, and I immersed in the mikveh. But we made a decision to observe a different time frame than the rebbitzen would have prescribed. The decision reflected awareness of the complicated process by which the separation period had become lengthened over thousands of years of observance.

It is striking that the way these laws are practiced today is not the way they appear in the related biblical passages; they are the outgrowth of two separate passages that were conflated by the rabbis of the Talmud.

The first passage appears amidst many rules regarding ritual purity that relay the ways a woman can become impure—*teme'ah*—and what it takes for her to return to the status of purity, *taharah*. The passage, Leviticus 15:19-33, appears in the context of a discussion of ritual impurity contracted by either male *or* female bodily emissions. Menstrual blood is one of the emissions that cause ritual impurity, or *tumah*. The passage begins like this:

> *When a woman has a discharge, her discharge being blood from her body, she shall remain in her ritual impurity seven days; whoever touches her shall be ritually impure until evening.*
> — Leviticus 15:19

This verse creates a week-long period of ritual impurity. What this verse doesn't do is command sexual abstinence during that period. Leviticus does not forbid contracting *tumah*, so there is no prohibition against touching a woman who is ritually impure. However, in Leviticus 15:24, we are told that if a man has sexual intercourse with a woman who is menstruating, he contracts the original *tumah*, including the same length of time – seven days – to be spent in that ritually impure state. In this case the man contracts the impurity on the same level that the woman has, as opposed to the lesser degree of *tumah* he contracts from, for example, merely sitting on a chair she has sat upon. Ritual impurity arising from indirect contact lasts only until the evening. However, when the man literally "touches" the actual source of the blood and thus the *tumah* through sexual intercourse, he contracts it as if he himself has bled.

It is clear that the Torah prefers ritual purity. Nevertheless, contracting *tumah* is not forbidden and was considered a natural, even if not desired, state to be in. People in biblical and Temple times probably avoided contracting *tumah* but if they did contract it, they dealt with it in the instructed ritual manner. However, from a practical point of view, ritual impurity primarily affected those who entered the Temple, and priests even outside the Temple, who needed to be pure to eat consecrated food. From the time of the destruction of the Temple and the subsequent cessation of priestly food gifts, ritual impurity has had no practical consequences.

Subsequent passages in Leviticus, however, show that *tumah* contracted from a blood flow from the uterus is more complex than other forms of ritual impurity. The context is two lists of forbidden acts (many of them sexual) that, if performed, prevent one from becoming *kadosh*, holy.

> *Do not come near a woman during her period of menstrual ritual impurity to uncover her nakedness.*
> — Leviticus 18:19

> *If a man lies with a woman during her infirmity and reveals her nakedness, he has laid bare her flow, and she has revealed the source of her blood flow; both of them shall be cut off from among their people.*
> — Leviticus 20:18

Taken together, these verses in Leviticus proscribe sexual relations during menstruation. The punishment of being "cut off" is called "*kareit*." The choice of the extraordinarily severe punishment in this context intensifies the taboo here more than a mere prohibition would.

It also explains why women still immerse today, after the destruction of the Temple, to reverse their impure status after menstruation but men do not do so after they contract impurity from seminal emissions. *Tumah* contracted from a uterine flow is the only ritual impurity that carries along with it a sexual prohibition and is therefore the only *tumah* that still has practical ramifications in our post-Temple reality. In order to resume sexual activity after becoming ritually impure from a uterine blood flow, women must immerse and reverse their ritually impure state—whether or not the Temple is standing.

Immersion in the mikveh isn't explicitly commanded. Rather, the Bible states that those who contract *tumat nidah* secondarily must wash. Proper washing was interpreted by the Rabbis to mean immersion in a collection of water called a mikveh. Ideally, a mikveh means either a natural body of water such as a spring, lake or ocean, or, if that is not possible, in a man-made pit filled with rain water. Today, for comfort and convenience purposes, communities build an institutional mikveh, a ritual bath with filtered and heated water that is connected to a rain water pit. (This way people immerse in the clean warm water instead of in the actual rain water pit, although it is as if they are immersing in the rain water pit since the two are connected; this is typical of rabbinic fictions invented by the Rabbis when they saw fit, to make Jewish practice more livable.[2]) The Rabbis also required the *nidah* (woman who has contracted impurity due to menstruation and who is considered a primary carrier of *tumah*) herself to immerse, since they assumed that if one who contracts *tumah* from a woman must wash, so must she.

Up until now, I have demarcated the basis of what may be termed "biblical *nidah*" practice: A seven day period of impurity and abstinence during menstruation, followed by immersion. This is what I practiced at the beginning of my marriage, dispensing with observance of the "clean" days that I first learned about in junior high—what is termed "rabbinic *nidah*" practice.

These extra days were added on when *nidah*, regular menstruation, was conflated with another type of uterine flow, irregular bleeding, described in the biblical verses that follow directly after those regarding menstrual impurity in Leviticus 15:

> *When a woman has had a discharge of blood for many days, not at the time of her menstrual period, or when she has a discharge beyond her menstrual period, she shall be ritually impure, as though at the time of her menstrual period, as long as her discharge lasts. Any bedding on which she lies while her discharge lasts shall be for her like bedding during her menstrual period; and any object on which she sits shall become ritually impure, as it does during her ritually impure menstrual period. Whoever touches them shall be ritually impure; he shall wash his clothes, bathe in water, and remain ritually impure until evening. When she becomes clean of her discharge, she counts*

---

[2] This is based on Leviticus 11:36, where we are told that a spring or collection of water in a pit does not contract *tumah*.

off seven days, and after that, she shall be ritually pure. On the
eighth day, she shall take two turtledoves or two pigeons, and
bring them to the priest and the entrance to the Tent of Meet-
ing... You shall put the Israelites on guard against their ritual
impurity, lest they die through their ritual impurity by defiling
my Tabernacle which is among them.
— Leviticus 15:19-32

This passage is about a woman who experiences an irregular blood flow for many days. (The Rabbis define this as a blood flow lasting three days or more not at the time of her regular period or a period that lasts for ten days or more.) When her blood flow stops, she counts another seven bloodless "clean" days (presumably to be sure the flow has stopped and she is cured of whatever caused this irregularity). At that time, she would bring a sacrificial offering before she could resume worship in the Temple. In Hebrew, the woman experiencing this flow is termed a *zavah* rather than a *nidah*. While the Torah does not explicitly prohibit intercourse with a *zavah*, rabbinic interpretation conflates the two and intercourse is forbidden for both.

These related laws raise a question: What determines whether a flow of blood is considered menstrual, *nidah*, or instead a non-menstrual, irregular flow, *zivah*, which has stricter rules? That is, how do we decide if the ordinary seven-day separation applies (counting from the first day the woman sees blood), or if the seven "clean" days must be added to the count?

According to the plain interpretation of the text, it seems the woman herself is the authority as to whether what she is experiencing is her period or not. But the Rabbis were not comfortable leaving matters in the hands of women, so they set in motion a series of amendments to the biblical rules that simplified matters by making them stricter.

First they defined *zivah* (the irregular uterine bleeding) as any uterine flow that occurs within eleven days of the cessation of regular menstrual bleeding. But it seems this was still too complex for women in the eyes of the Rabbis, and thus began a further series of stringencies. Rabbi Judah the Prince began this trend by declaring that all women experiencing a

flow of blood from their uterus must relate to this flow with the strictest case scenario. This means that if she bleeds for one or two days, she
must treat the flow as a regular "*nidah*" period and wait a total of seven
days[3], and if she bleeds for three or more days, she waits until the flow
stops and then counts seven clean days (treating the flow as an irregular
"*zivah*" flow). Later, Rabbi Zeira (although he based his move on the fact
that women were already being stringent on themselves in this manner)
ratified this stricture by completely conflating *nidah* with *zivah* and ruling that a woman who sees even one drop of blood must wait the seven
clean days.

During our first few years of marriage, Jacob and I refrained from
sexual activity during the seven days required for menstruation by biblical law (counting from the first show of blood). We did not keep the
seven extra "clean" days required by rabbinic law (counting from when
the bleeding stops). This meant that when I was experiencing a regular menstrual period, we refrained from sex and all sexual activity for
seven days. On the night of the seventh day (which is the beginning of
the eighth day according to Jewish Law, since a "Jewish day" goes from
sundown to sundown not sunrise to sunrise) I would immerse in the
mikveh and we would resume our sexual relationship. After an unusual
uterine flow, I would perform an internal examination, which consisted
of inserting a clean, dry cloth into the vaginal canal to make sure the
bleeding had indeed stopped. If the cloth came out clean, I would count
seven clean days, doing internal checks at the beginning and end of the
seven days to make sure the bleeding did not start again. During this
entire period Jacob and I refrained from sexually intimate interactions,
as with a regular menstrual period.

As a religious feminist, this was my compromise with this ritual. I kept
the laws according to the Torah, treating my judgment of my own body
with more respect than that accorded to it by the rabbis of the Talmud.

---

[3] This is considered a stringency because according to the rabbinic interpretation of
biblical *zivah*, a flow of one or two days requires only one "clean" day. Only a flow of
three or more days requires seven "clean" days.

I saw the rabbinic strictures surrounding the laws of *nidah* (and *zivah*) as reflecting a general distrust of women and disgust with women's bodies, especially uterine blood. I was especially uncomfortable with the Rabbis' equating regular menstruation with an unnatural uterine blood flow that could be an indication of illness. Moreover, I resented their patronizing attitude toward women, assuming that we could not tell the difference. But I was well aware of the biblical prohibition and felt committed to keeping these laws in some form.

The idea of monthly immersions in the mikveh appealed to me. I liked the spiritual aspect of a monthly renewal ritual, especially one that included water. (A daily swimmer, I have always felt drawn to water.)

It was difficult for Jacob and me to curb our sexual urges on the days when sex was forbidden to us, but the regular separations made our lovemaking all the more intense. Expressing our love in non-physical ways proved a helpful skill for our relationship. And we learned to resolve arguments (at least during those times of the month) with actual solutions rather than always diffusing the tension through sex.

Four years after we were married, as part of my studies for rabbinic ordination, I studied the laws of *nidah* daily for an entire academic year. By that time, Jacob and I had begun following the rabbinic interpretation of these laws, which is the mainstream Orthodox approach. This was part of a general theological shift I had made at that point in my life from a more critical feminist approach to Jewish Law to a more accommodating approach. I saw myself as making compromises for tradition in order to slowly work for feminist change from within the system. That is how I ended up at the all-women's yeshiva where I began my studies for ordination (although at this institution the studies were not defined as such).

I learned directly from the original rabbinic sources about the halakhic (Jewish legal) development of these laws, how the passages of Leviticus were interpreted in talmudic times and in later rabbinic rulings. It was disturbing to find texts about women's biology written exclusively by men, but the fact that these texts were often misogynist and medically inaccurate made matters worse. My earlier feminist suspicions were confirmed: Much of the development of the laws of *nidah* stemmed from the ancient rabbis' negative ideas about women, their bodies, their blood, and what the rabbis saw as their essentially simple-minded nature.

That year I developed a strategy that lasted throughout my rabbinic studies: academic detachment. I told myself that these texts belonged to a certain time and place. This detachment did not carry over into my observance of the ritual. Counting days and separating from my husband gave me a heightened awareness of my biology and its cyclical nature. I still cherished my monthly mikveh immersions. The ritual was meaningful to me in my time and my place, regardless of its origins in the unflattering rabbinic opinion of women.

I experienced the laws of *nidah* as challenging, but not oppressive. They served to elevate my life in many ways. I continued to keep these laws as interpreted by the Rabbis and began teaching them to women and couples before their weddings. I was so fascinated with this topic that I began writing my doctoral dissertation on it a few years later.

While writing my dissertation I began to understand that the picture was more complicated than I had realized. It was not enough for me to reinterpret this ritual for myself. There were aspects of the ritual as it developed and was understood and applied over time that were so deeply entrenched in misogynist interpretations that their very practice perpetuated ideologies that are harmful to women's psyches and self-image.

Take *tumah*, ritual impurity: The fact that the only *tumah* ritual still enforced today is associated with the blood flow from a woman's uterus has negatively influenced the perception—by both men and women—of women and their bodies. All *tumah* ideology and associations after the Temple's destruction have been focused upon the bleeding woman; therefore, today, women (and only women) are perceived to have the biological capacity to become ritually impure. The Jewish legal and spiritual reality is that both men and women still to this day contract *tumah*, but it is only women who contract *tumah* from uterine bleeding who are obliged to immerse, since only this *tumah* carries with it a sexual prohibition. Some men still immerse in the mikveh, but not out of an obligation to reverse their status of ritual impurity. Rather they immerse for the spiritual experience; therefore, their immersions are not associated in the collective subconscious with ritual impurity in the way that women's immersions are. One could even say that *tumah* consciousness has disappeared today in relation to men but not in relation to women.

Since the destruction of the Temple, *tumat nidah* has been interpreted in misogynist ways. It has been specifically understood by Jewish scholars and authorities, as well as by the mass culture, as being a lower spiritual state, connected to filth and danger—antithetical to the holy. These characteristics have, in turn, been associated with women in general, regardless of their state, because all women are potential bleeders.

We cannot escape the integral connection between *tumah* and *nidah*. A woman's sexual status is dependent upon her *tumah* status. In most halakhic sources on this topic, the status of the woman is referred to as either *teme'ah* or *tehorah*, even though the issue at hand in this post-Temple era is whether or not the woman is permitted to be sexually active and not whether she will be able to worship in the Temple, or eat sacrifices.

To make matters worse, both folk practices of *nidah* and halakhic and philosophical writings on the subject continue to apply practices, concepts, and terminology of ritual impurity in the context of women's uterine bleeding as though the Temple were still standing. For example, despite the fact that *tumah* should no longer be of practical concern in a post-Temple reality, prominent halakhic authorities in the Middle Ages reinforced *tumah*-avoidance practices in relation to the woman in *nidah*. We have responsa in which Jewish men wrote to the halakhic authorities of the time, asking if they could stop avoiding their wives when they were in *nidah*, now that these men had no reason to be concerned about the consequences of contracting their wives' *tumah*. While their wives were off-limits to them sexually because of their impure status, the threat of contagion was no longer an issue, since contracting *tumah* would have no practical ramifications for the men themselves.

The answer these men received, in writing, was that they should continue to avoid their wives because, although they were correct that contracting their wives' *tumah* was no longer a problem, it was best to keep their distance in order to prevent being sexually aroused. These *tumah*-related distancing practices, which were then officially integrated into the system of intimacy-related (not *tumah*-related) distancing practices (or "*harchakot*") already existent in the Talmud, often alienate women in *nidah* and make them feel that they are being avoided out of fear of contamination rather than from a mutually agreed upon desire to limit contact that is sexually arousing.

It is not only in relation to her husband that a woman in *nidah* is made to feel alienated. Despite the clear lack of halakhic basis for it, there are a host of strong customs of distancing women in *nidah* or *zivah* from sacred objects and holy spaces. A good example of this is the notion that a menstruating woman should not touch a Torah scroll or, in some communities, even enter a synagogue at all. There is no basis for these customs other than misogyny and blood taboo. A Torah scroll cannot contract *tumah*, and men too are ritually impure from seminal emissions, even though they are not obligated to immerse in order to remove these ritual impurities in order to have sexual relations.

This and other similar folk customs have been reinforced by major halakhic authorities. Rabbi Moshe Isserles, who wrote the authoritative Ashkenazic gloss on the Shulkhan Aruch, wrote that although technically there is no problem with a woman entering a synagogue, it is the custom for women to remain outside the synagogue when menstruating. While this extreme custom is rarely enforced today, its spirit is being perpetuated. Stories abound of contemporary rabbis telling their congregations that women can have a Torah scroll to dance with on Simchat Torah on the condition that menstruating women not touch it!

And in the realm of language, most current day *nidah* manuals use *tumah* terminology, and some mikveh attendants will even declare a woman "*tehorah*" after she immerses properly in the mikveh. This type of continued use of *tumah* terminology in itself is not harmful, and it is certainly not inaccurate; however, without positive feminist reinterpretations of *tumah* dominating the general social consciousness, applying *tumah* terminology in the context of a modern-day menstruating woman can be extremely damaging.

Some feminists, such as Reform Jewish theologian Rachel Adler, have argued that the most effective remedy to this problem would be to let go of the rituals around *nidah* and *zivah* all together.[4] Keeping these practices alive perpetuates *tumah* consciousness around women, after all. If we discontinue these practices, associations between women and *tumah* will eventually disappear. Even if we re-interpret *tumah* in positive feminist ways, *tumat nidah* and its associated rituals are already so loaded with negative misogynist baggage that they are irredeemable. *Tumah* remains alive only in so much as we keep it alive, and it is best that we bury the concept altogether at this point, she argues.

But it is not as simple as that. The matter is made more complex because of the inextricable link between *tumah* and the sexual prohibition related to a uterine flow. Is the ritually-conscious Jewish world ready to let go of this sexual prohibition, or is this sexual taboo around menstruation still alive in our cultural reality? There are many couples who naturally refrain from sex when a woman is menstruating, not only because some men are turned off by the blood, but also because there are many women who enjoy that time when their bodies are completely their own. Perhaps there are too many positive gains from a rhythmic sexual relationship to abandon this ritual. While some religious feminists have advocated for doing away with this ritual altogether, others have suggested reclaiming and reinterpreting it. They emphasize the ritual's potential to sanctify sexuality and to connect women with their bodies in a positive way.[5]

On one hand, *nidah* is a ritual that — particularly as interpreted in a culture dominated by men — has caused harm to women's perceptions

---

[4] See her article, "In Your Blood, Live: ReVisions of a Theology of Purity," *Tikkun*, vol. 8, no. 1, Jan./Feb. 1993.

[5] Rachel Adler is one of them. In a famous article titled "Tumah and Taharah: Ends and Beginnings" that she wrote for *The Jewish Catalog* in 1972, when she identified as an Orthodox Jewish feminist, she argued that *tumat nidah* is a spiritual opportunity for women to connect to the cycle of life and death and face their own mortality through the natural cycles and rhythms of their bodies.

of themselves as both physical and spiritual beings. On the other hand, however, it is a ritual that focuses on the woman and her body and therefore has the potential, when interpreted in a positive, feminist way, to be a source of spiritual expression and fulfillment for women.

In fact, the immersion ritual in general has incredible power to mark transformation and renewal. So rather than throw the mitzvah out with the mikveh waters, I have in my own life chosen to seek ways to reclaim *nidah* and mikveh. I have, for myself, transformed them into a source of empowerment and spiritual enrichment, rather than a cause of degradation and a spiritual drain.

The Bible—II Kings, chapter 3—relates how, in the days of Elisha the prophet, three kings set out to conquer Moab: the king of Israel, the king of Judah, and the king of Edom. When they reached the tip of the Dead Sea, the troops ran out of water. They summoned Elisha the prophet, who brought down the Hand of God, and the wadi was filled with pools of water. In the morning, more water came from the direction of Edom—which is from the root of the word "*adom*," which means red in Hebrew—and the land was covered with water.

When the Moabites heard they were being attacked, they looked in the direction of the three armies. The red morning sun was shining over the water, and the water looked to them like blood.

"That's blood!" they said. "The kings must have fought among themselves and killed one another. Now to the spoils, Moab!"

In the end, it was the three armies—of Israel, Judah, and Edom—who collected the spoils of Moab, and the king of Moab offered his son as a sacrifice to appease his gods.

Years later, in the time of the Talmud, the scholar Rav is asked how we know blood must be red to be considered *nidah* blood. He answers by citing the verse from this story: "The Moabites saw the water over against them as red as blood."[6]

---

[6] BT Shabbat 108a

❧ ❧ ❧

Since Pesach, the members of my CHaNaH group had been immersing ourselves in the mitzvah of *nidah*. We had used up our flour, put
away our chametzdik challah bowls and mixing spoons, and moved on
to studying together the mitzvot of *nidah* and mikveh.

We studied some of the laws of *nidah*, shared our own "blood stories,"
and discussed our feelings about menstruation and its attendant rituals.
Each of us had different feelings about both of these topics. Some of us
had positive experiences of our first periods to relay, while others had
traumatic ones. Some of us loved keeping the laws of *nidah,* and others resented keeping them. Some kept the rabbinic laws of *nidah*, while
some kept the biblical laws, while some did not keep the laws at all.
Two women in the group used to keep the laws, but were now post-
menopause. Both said that in some ways they missed the experience, but
in other ways, they were happy to let it go.

Now that summer was upon us, the weather was getting warmer, and
we had delved into *nidah* and mikveh on both an intellectual and emotional level, we decided that it was time to move on to the spiritual level
and have a group mikveh experience. So we planned an excursion to a
nearby natural mikveh. It was a warm Friday morning in June. As the
sun rose in the sky, heating up the still-cool desert sand, we headed off
on a hike into a wadi that was a twenty-minute drive from our neighborhood. The hike ended in a series of natural pools of water that would be
ideal for ritual immersion.

We reached the first pool of water, down in the wadi, stripped to our
bathing suits and jumped in. The water was cold, but not unpleasant, and
when we were sure there was no one else around, we removed our suits
and immersed one by one. For me and another friend, this was actually
the time of the month when we needed to immerse, so together we said
the blessing on ritual immersion. Three other women—two who had
not immersed in the mikveh since they had stopped menstruating over
ten years before and another who had not been to the mikveh since the
day before her wedding more than twenty years before—felt moved to
say the Shehechianu, the blessing on new things and experiences. And

the remaining two women simply immersed without a blessing, as is the practice for non-obligatory ritual immersions.

We stayed in the water for a while, splashing and singing. As we did, I noticed that the sun was hitting the water in such a way that it took on a reddish tint. We were in the desert, the place of mirage. I could have sworn the water looked like blood. Not pure thick blood, but a blood-water mixture. I thought of the story of how, at Elisha's request, God had miraculously filled the wadi with pools of water, and how the Moabites mistook the water for blood; and how, years later, Rav derived from this story the color of uterine blood.

Rav's interpretation had always puzzled me. I did not understand his association between this story and *nidah* blood. After all, the blood in this story is the blood of war, the blood of death and child sacrifice. To me, these associations with blood seemed so far removed from uterine blood, which I saw as life-giving, life-nurturing. This story is violent, and so, I had assumed his interpretation was violent as well. In my mind, Rav connected menstrual blood with killing and destruction. He saw the menstrual flow through the eyes of the King of Moab, to whom it was like a Sea of Blood—literally a blood bath. Therefore, when I had read this midrash in the past, it had offended me.

Immersing with my friends that morning, however, I began to think that Rav was missing the point of the biblical story: the close connection between blood and water. Both are symbolic of life. Blood is understood as the symbol of life in the Bible; therefore, we are forbidden to eat the blood of an animal. Water (which makes up seventy percent of the human body and without which we cannot live) is referred to in the Bible in the context of its power as a tool of ritual purification as "*mayim hayyim,*" living waters. *Tumah* is associated with death in the Bible; and thus, "living waters" are an obvious way to reverse one's *tumah* state.

Menstrual blood, however, is one cause of *tumah,* and *tumah* is associated with death. Since water is what rids one of *tumah,* blood and water can be seen as antithetical—water being associated with life and blood being associated with death. So I should not have been surprised by Rav's morbid associations with menstrual blood. It was just that I, a woman, saw it differently. For me, uterine blood meant life. In my mind, the reason a flow of blood from the uterus causes *tumah* is not that blood is associated with death, but that the loss of that blood (a symbol of life) from the body is associated with death. Therefore, when I thought of a Sea of Blood, I thought of the mixture of two symbols of life: blood and water. This image was for me beautiful, not frightening or threatening.

It seemed to me now that this biblical story also presented water and blood as sources of life. It was a matter of point of view. God saves the soldiers with water. But the king of Moab saw only the blood in his perception of the water and death in his perception of the blood. This was his downfall. And Rav too fell into this trap. He saw the blood through the Moabite king's eyes.

Then it occurred to me that perhaps I was misjudging Rav. Perhaps his midrashic interpretation of this story was more complex than I was giving him credit for. Could it be that Rav chose this specific story to determine the color of *nidah* blood because of its association between blood and water? After all, the *nidah* ritual includes both of these liquids. Perhaps Rav too saw the connection between menstrual blood, water, and life. Perhaps he is actually critiquing rather than echoing the Moabite King's point-of-view. After all, he could have chosen any image of blood in biblical literature. There is no lack of blood in the Bible. Nevertheless, he chose this story—a strange choice, considering what the Moabites saw was not really blood at all, but water.

On the other hand, the ramification of blood being labeled *nidah* blood is that it renders the woman *teme'ah*, ritually impure. *Tumah*, ritual impurity, has direct associations with death. So perhaps I was reading Rav too generously.

Either way, now, as I splashed and sang with my friends in this wadi, I loved the image of this Sea of Blood. As I immersed in the water, I imagined that I was immersing in my own uterine blood, the life-sustaining uterine lining that had protected and nourished each of my five children for nine whole months in my womb. Mikveh immersion had always felt to me like a return to the womb, but until now, this image had been totally pristine for me. I had imagined myself floating in clear amniotic fluid. Somehow, the blood of the uterus had been removed from the picture. But now, I embraced that blood.

I imagined the blood mixing with the water, and I was reminded of the word used in the biblical creation story for the pre-creation waters, the "*tehom.*" In ancient Babylonian mythology, the goddess Tiamat is identified with the "salty waters," which are associated both with the ocean and with menstrual blood. She has been called the "Ocean of Blood."[7] She is the Red Sea. The Arabic name for the eastern shore of the Red Sea is *Tihamat.* I imagined us, a group of women, splashing in this watery, bloody *tehom.*

As we have seen, there is a false perception among Jewish religious practitioners (and even non-practitioners) that only women's bodies are sources of *tumah* today—this despite the rabbinic approach that *tumah* in general did not disappear from the world. In fact, one could even understand *tumah* as being even more rampant than ever, since *tumah* that is caused by certain sinful behaviors (one of which is intercourse with a *nidah*) is understood to be a cause of the national exile. The truth is that *tumah* today is merely ignored in most cases. Except that of the bleeding woman.

This perception of women as impure is ironic, because women who go to the mikveh today on a regular basis are less ritually impure than men, who remain in their state of *tumah* (such as that caused by seminal emissions) indefinitely if they do not immerse. Some men choose to immerse before Yom Kippur or Shabbat, but the majority never immerse at all.

Nonetheless, women are seen on a subconscious societal level as the source of *tumah.* This is especially true for unmarried women, because traditionally women only begin immersing in the mikveh when they marry. Therefore, from the time a woman begins to menstruate until she is married and begins to immerse in the mikveh, she is seen as perpetually *teme'ah.*

One can imagine, then, that the onset of a young woman's menses is no cause for celebration in the traditional Jewish world, to say the least. This is exacerbated by the fact that no traditional Jewish ritual exists marking

---

[7]Judy Grahn, *Blood, Bread, and Roses: How Menstruation Created the World*, p. 9.

the onset of menstruation. This pivotal moment in a woman's life is at best ignored, and at worst understood, at least on a subconscious level, as the moment in her life when she went from being pure to impure, from *tehorah* to *teme'ah*, a condition that will only be reversed, if she chooses to remain within the traditional norm, when she immerses in the mikveh and becomes legally sexually permitted in the context of marriage.

Becoming a woman, then, means becoming the opposite of holy. Can one imagine a worse message to send a young woman?

This is why it is so important to me to create positive reinterpretations of the transition between *tumah* to *taharah* related to a woman's uterine flow. Rather than ignore *tumah*, which is an integral part of the laws and rituals surrounding this flow, my approach is to address it through feminist reinterpretation, and through creating rituals with positive connotations surrounding noteworthy occasions of uterine flow.

When my oldest daughter Michal menstruated for the first time, I felt a need to counteract the negative *tumah* energy inevitably associated with this event. I had read women's accounts of how they experienced the onset of menstruation, and some of these "blood stories" were quite shocking. As a mother of three daughters, I felt responsible for what their "blood stories" would be. I did not want to miss this opportunity to affect my daughter's relationship with her body. I explained to her why I thought it so important that we celebrate and that we do so among her friends. She had the power to influence others and share this experience with them, I told her. It seems my argument was convincing enough, because Michal agreed to let me throw her a slumber party with her closest friends in honor of the onset of her menses.

During the holiday of Sukkot, Jacob, Adin and Nachum (who by then was weaned) went camping on the beach in Tel-Aviv, while Michal, Meira, Hallel, and I, and about seven eleven- and twelve-year-old girls, slept out in the sukkah, colored our hair and painted our bodies with natural henna, and watched the movie "Thirteen Going on Thirty" (Michal's choice, and while it was not my idea of a good film, the coming-of-age theme was appropriate, and it certainly went over big with the girls!).

Before the movie, we sat around a table and each guest offered a blessing to Michal. As each girl spoke, she strung beautiful red beads on a wire that became a necklace for Michal. Some were shy and said no more than a quick "*mazal tov!*" (which in itself is overcoming a huge hurdle in recognizing that this event is a cause for congratulations!). But a surprising number truly spoke from their hearts. One girl in particular brought tears to my eyes when she told Michal that she was jealous of her, because she got her period, which means that she is now a woman and can bring children into the world.

As we placed the beads on the wire, it was as if we were stringing our blessings onto this necklace that would forever be a memento for Michal of this magical evening. And as we blessed Michal, we munched on pomegranate seeds and pieces of heart-shaped, blood-red sponge cake. Meira, Hallel, and I had baked the cake without Michal and covered it with white frosting (I decided to make an exception to my usual no-food-coloring rule for this unique purpose). The red color was to be a surprise. And Michal was certainly surprised. When she cut into the cake, the red inner part glimmered like blood.

I hope to never forget the look in her eyes as she cut into that cake. "That was the coolest cake ever!" she said and gave me a big hug when all of her friends left in the morning, each with a red heart-shaped box of heart-shaped chocolates in hand. "Actually, that was the coolest party ever. I'm glad we did it. Thanks, *Ima*."

It certainly was a night to remember, which was precisely the point. I was hoping these friends would choose to do the same at the onset of their menses (my daughter was the first among her friends to get her period). They didn't. But there is not one girl who was present that night who was not changed even in some subtle way by the experience. Of that I am sure. And most importantly, Michal will have this as her "blood story" to share with her children, God willing, some day.

(When my second daughter, Meira, got her period six years later, we had already moved to a kibbutz in northern Israel, where I run the mikveh. We held Meira's period party in the mikveh building, and she did a moving immersion ritual with Michal and me in the room, before her friends strung her red beaded necklace.[8])

---

[8] For more on my second daughter Meira's "period party" five years later, see my article in Zeek at http://zeek.forward.com/articles/117283/ .

❧ ❧ ❧

In rabbinic usage, the term "*mitamtem*" means to block. In Tractate Pesahim 42a, a fatty dairy food is said to block, *mitamtem*, the heart, and in Tractate Yoma 39a, sin is also said to block, *mitamtem*, the heart. In this last source, the midrash actually uses as a proof text Leviticus 11:43. The context is forbidden foods, and the author of the midrash does a word play on *timtum* and *tumah*. Rabbinic literature thus makes a connection between *tumah* and blockage.

I have found that this is how I experience being in the state of *tumah*. It is a time when the boundary-setting side of me is stronger. And while this may close me off in ways, even spiritual ways, setting boundaries is a necessary part of being able to function – in my relationship with Jacob in particular, but also in all of my relationships. In fact, setting boundaries is a necessary part of being able to function in the world.

There is something that works for me in the together/apart cycle inherent in the *nidah* ritual. It speaks to my need to balance the two sides of myself that are both very strong but also seemingly contradictory: my willing side and my willful side, my open side and my closed side, my externally-directed side and my internally-directed side, my giving side and my boundary-building side, or, in the antimony of the Kabbalah, my side of *hessed*, mercy, and my side of *gevurah*, strength.

Living a life conscious of *tumah* and *taharah* is about being aware of these two sides of myself and making room for them to exist simultaneously in my life. This consciousness allows for both of these approaches to exist within the same relationship, and allows for both of these ways of being in the world to exist within me. While it may seem best to have these two sides both constantly present and in balance, the *nidah* cycle promotes a more realistic model that may even be healthier in the long run. Instead of complete equanimity, this approach promotes fluctuation. Sometimes my *gevurah* side is dominant, and sometimes my *hessed* side is dominant. And this is fine, as long as each is given its appropriate time to dominate.

It's not as though when I am in *nidah* I am always closed and self-absorbed, and when I am not in *nidah*, I am always open and giving. But perhaps I *am* more inclined in one direction than the other depending on my *nidah* status. Perhaps when I am *teme'ah*, I *am* more closed, and when I am *tehorah*, I *am* more open. But I think the cycle for me is less literal than that. I think it is about recognizing that I have both of these elements within me, and that this is okay, as long as they are kept at a balance that is beneficial to my growth, rather than detrimental to it.

This manifests itself in a more literal way in my relationship with Jacob. When I am in *nidah*, I am less open to him, at least in a physical way. My physical boundaries influence the general energy I project. And when I am not in *nidah*, I must send off signals that are more willing and available in general. We all fluctuate in our degrees of readiness to give and receive. But what this rhythm does is regulate these swings so that they do not go out of control in either direction.

This cycle gives me a healthy amount of time to live in my *gevurah*-minded mode when I tend to be more willful, and then in my *hessed*-minded mode when I tend to be more willing. By living out this cycle, the two sides are kept in a general balance. And while it may be harder for Jacob to deal with the side of me that is *gevurah* (boundary-building) and while it may be more difficult for him to be in our relationship when I am in *nidah*, he loves me even then. And that is important for me to know.

Tumah is only harmful if it is not given its healthy time to exist and then be reversed to *taharah*, its flip side, the side that opens us up so spiritual energy can flow in. But *taharah* too must have its end, its chance to be dormant in us so that *tumah* can return once again. Just as too much *gevurah* can be a bad thing, so can too much *hessed*. The two must learn to make room for each other at the proper time.

This sense is especially strong for me when I am trying to conceive. When my period comes, I turn inward. I am disappointed, even saddened, by the loss of potential life inside me. I may even become resentful. I need my space to grieve, and that is what I get. Days and days of *tumah* space. And then, when the time comes to return to the *tehorah* state, I welcome immersion in water as a way to transition from one state into another. I return to the womb, to that safe fluid space where everything and anything seems possible and where I can reconnect with my spiritual center, and I am filled once again with hope. My spirit is renewed. And I am reborn, refreshed, and ready to try again. I am open to receive God's blessings or to be hurt once again.

This is one aspect of what it means for me to be in a state of *tumah* from my uterine flow. For other women, no doubt, the experience is different. We are all entitled to our own private meanings of the *nidah* ritual. But in order for the ritual to survive in an authentic and sincere way, it is our responsibility as women to reclaim this ritual and reinterpret it, express what it means for us in the 21st century to be *temeot* from our uterine blood. For too many centuries, we have let men tell us what this means. Menstruating women have been seen in rabbinic sources as dangerous, filthy, sinful, and profane as a result of their *tumah*. It is about time that we take matters into our own hands.

> *Said Rav Yosef said Rav Yehudah said Rav: Rebbe [Rabbi Judah the Prince] issued an edict in the outskirts: If a woman sees one day of bleeding, she should wait six days plus that one day; if she sees two days of bleeding, she should wait six/five[9] days plus those two days; if she sees three days of bleeding, she should wait seven clean days [plus those three days]. Said Rabbi Zeira: The daughters of Israel were stringent upon themselves; even when they saw a drop of blood the size of a mustard seed, they waited the seven clean days.*
> — BT Nidah 66a

The Bible clearly distinguishes between the *nidah*, the woman with a regular menstrual flow, and the *zavah*, the woman with an irregular menstrual flow. According to biblical law, the *nidah* is automatically in a state of *tumah* for a total of seven days from the time she starts bleeding, as long as her flow lasts for seven days or fewer. If her flow lasts for ten or more days[10], or if she bleeds for three days or more during a time when

---

[9] There are two different versions of this text.

[10] If her menstrual period lasts for eight or nine days she is a *zavah ketana* and need wait only one day after the flow stops before she can immerse.

she is not expecting her regular period[11], she is a *zavah gedolah* and must wait until her flow stops and then count seven clean days before she can immerse and resume relations.

In the late tanaitic period, the *nidah* was conflated with the *zavah*. According to rabbinic law, any woman who bleeds from her uterus—whether it is during the time she expects her period, or whether it is for one day, three days, or fourteen days—must wait a minimum of four days if she is of Sephardic descent and five days if she is of Ashkenazic descent[12], then perform a *hefsek taharah* (an internal check, to determine that the bleeding has in fact stopped), and then wait seven clean days before she immerses in the mikveh and resumes sexual relations. In other words, rabbinic law turned a healthy menstruating woman into a sickly woman experiencing an irregular flow.

What does this say about the way the rabbis view the bleeding woman? If all women are *zavot*, then our bleeding is not normal; it is sickly, irregular, and therefore dangerous and frightening. Even threatening. It is not natural. It is not part of the regular ways of nature. This stricture, it seems, came mostly as a reaction to and categorization of women's menstrual blood as dangerous and abnormal. Men conflated these two very different experiences because of their lack of ability to relate to the idea that blood can flow, even in seemingly large amounts, and not be a cause for concern. In fact, the Rabbis may have been influenced by the Zoroastrians who saw all uterine blood as a cause for concern. I can't help but wonder whether the Rabbis' thought process went something like this: *Wouldn't we men be better off if all women wait a week before we enter their dark, bloody places again? Let's wait until we are sure the coast is clear and all blood is gone before we even go near them again!*

But women live with this blood. We know the difference.

What, then, does it mean when we are told that it was the "daughters of Israel" who took this stringency upon themselves? In the Babylonian

---

[11] If she bleeds for one or two days at a time when she is not expecting her regular period (which the Rabbis interpret to mean within eighteen days after her period started), she is also a *zavah ketana*.

[12] Formally, to be sure that any semen that may be left in her reproductive tract from intercourse has lost its potency and therefore its ability to pass on *tumah*, although it seems the motive of the Rabbis may have been to discourage repeated sexual intercourse so soon after bleeding after intercourse.

Talmud, we learn that it was Rabbi Judah the Prince, the compiler of the Mishnah, who initiated this move towards conflating *nidah* and *zivah* when he made timing of the blood flow a non-issue. With his edict, it no longer mattered if the flow occurred when a woman was expecting her period or not; all blood was treated as the strictest scenario. In fact, the Talmud (in tractate Nidah 67b) also refers to "the Rabbis" as being the ones who put all bleeding women into the category of "*safek zavot*," presumed *zavot*.

But it was the women themselves, "the daughters of Israel," who took upon themselves the final stricture that they would wait seven clean days even for a tiny drop of blood. According to this source, what the women did was make the amount of blood and number of days of the flow a non-issue.

I understand how women may have wanted to make their lives easier by cooperating with an approach that creates one rule for all bleeding. Convenience is a strong motivating factor when it comes to ritual and law. Alternatively, perhaps these women saw this act as a form of birth control. At the time of the Talmud, the common belief was that a woman is most fertile right after she stops bleeding. In their eyes, tacking on seven more days of abstinence would have decreased the chances of conception. Or, this could have been an act of independence in another way: Lengthening this period could have been a way for these women to abstain from sexual relations with their husbands at a time when women did not have much power or free choice in their marital relationships.

This is all conjecture. We can never know why the "daughters of Israel" cooperated with the Rabbis in their move towards stricture in this area or—if one may dare say so—whether they really did or not. In any event, treating all women today as presumed *zavot* takes this matter out of the hands of women. It is a statement that women cannot be trusted to judge when their blood flow is normal or abnormal. Even if the rabbinic system is simpler, it dis-empowers women and creates a situation where all uterine blood—whether or not it is the result of a normal menstrual period—is treated as an infirmity. Even if women in talmudic times saw benefit in adding an extra seven clean days after a normal menstrual period, it is difficult for women in the 21st century to relate to this move.

The question therefore is: Must we continue to toe the rabbinic line in this area, or can we take back the power to name our own blood?

In medieval Egypt, there were women who objected to keeping the extra seven clean days when they were experiencing what was clearly a regular menstrual period. In fact, it seems that there was a mass move among these women not only to return to keeping the biblical *nidah* laws in terms of the number of days they would separate from their husbands, but they also did not immerse in a proper mikveh. Instead, they would sprinkle water upon one another.

In a halakhic responsum[13] of Rabbi Moshe ben Maimon (also known as Maimonides), who lived in 14th century Spain and then Egypt, we are told of an edict that was sent out by the rabbinic authorities of the time declaring that any woman who refused to keep the seven clean days and immerse in a proper halakhic mikveh could be divorced by her husband without her *ketubah* money. This meant that she would, in most cases, be sent out into the street penniless. This put an end to this woman's revolution. But not all "daughters of Israel," it seems, were willing to submit to this rabbinic stricture without a fight.

Early on in mine and Jacob's marriage, I decided that I could live with the rabbinic version of these laws. I could tolerate waiting the extra seven days in all cases in order to not break with this long-standing rabbinic tradition. I could even find benefits in keeping a longer period of sexual abstinence. I told myself that if our sex life was enhanced by one week of abstinence, how much more so would it by a two-week waiting period! And if having a time with no physical communication helped us strengthen our verbal communication skills, wouldn't it be wise to have two weeks like this each month, thus keeping the physical and the non-physical in equal balance?

---

[13] *Teshuvot HaRambam* 242, 434-444

But mostly, my decision to return to the rabbinic framework was because I did not feel that straying from the tradition and the communal norm was justified in my case. I did not consider waiting those extra seven days an unbearable sacrifice and I had convinced myself that perhaps the women did indeed cooperate for a good reason.

But then, after I weaned Nachum, I began to have shorter menstrual cycles, until it reached the point where I found it difficult to conceive. I was ovulating before I even went to the mikveh. I began sharing my dilemma with other women, and I discovered that this problem was not unique to me. It even has a name: "halakhic infertility." As most women age, their periods tend to be shorter and their ovulation time earlier. Therefore, halakhic infertility is even more common now than ever, since women are having children later in life than they ever have before.

The common "treatment" of halakhic infertility is to delay ovulation with hormones. And if that does not work, artificial insemination is used—the rationale being that it is sexual intercourse that is forbidden, not inserting sperm into a woman's cervix. On one hand, these seem like the easiest, most practical solutions to the problem. On the other hand, however, these women are not sick. There is nothing wrong with them. Their menstrual cycle simply does not jibe with the requirements of rabbinic law. What is the problem: these women's cycles or the halakhah? That, for me, was the question.

It seemed that rabbinic authorities prefer to manipulate a woman's cycle with hormones, or even insert her husband's sperm in a medical procedure, rather than create a halakhic solution. With the biblical principle of *"pru urvu,"* be fruitful and multiply, pitted against the rabbinic principle of treating normal menstruation like abnormal bleeding, how can rabbinic authorities make the latter a higher priority—especially when the Torah does make a clear distinction between *nidah* and *zavah* and how they should be treated?

Why do Orthodox rabbinic authorities like Rabbi Moshe Feinstein maintain the conflation of *nidah* with *zivah* even in a case where the woman would not be able to conceive naturally otherwise? The reason Rabbi Feinstein gives is that this is an ancient law that goes all the way back to the early talmudic period.[14] Is this formalistic answer what is truly at the heart of his decision? What is he really saying as he protects this law so vehemently, even at the expense of these women? It seems he is afraid that if this rabbinic enactment falls, all of tradition, all of Torah as we know it, will fall. But why? What is so precious about these seven clean days? Why are *poskim* today so attached to treating all bleeding women as *zavot*?

Perhaps even the Orthodox rabbinic authorities of today are uneasy about the idea of having intercourse with a woman right after she has stopped bleeding. They want those seven extra clean days as a safety net against sin to ensure that women are indeed blood-free before they are permitted to resume sex; or perhaps they still can't relate to the idea that menstruation is a totally natural phenomenon that is not a reflection of something wrong with a woman or her body.

Or maybe they are unwilling to bend on this issue because it means trusting women to differentiate between normal and abnormal bleeding, and they are unwilling to put that power into women's hands—especially because the biblical punishment for both the women and their husbands is so severe if they do end up having intercourse at the wrong time.

Or could it be that they are simply protecting the status quo in general? They may be assuming that if they bend on this issue, the whole hierarchical system that places rabbis at the top, lay men below them, and women below them, will fall apart, and with that, the entire religion will crumble. It is also possible that they feel that a change such as this in Jewish practice would create too much of a rupture with the past, with tradition, and with the textual sources, and would therefore create an atmosphere of laissez faire halakhah that could end up destroying Torah as we know it.

As I examined all of these possible explanations, I wondered if I could continue to keep the seven clean days after experiencing a regular menstrual period. Perhaps these rabbis are correct. Perhaps instituting such a change could threaten Torah as we know it. But was I prepared to preserve the halakhic system at all costs? Was I willing to cooperate with a halakhic system that continually claims the need to preserve tradition by

---

[14] *Igrot Moshe*, Yoreh Deah, 1:93

sacrificing its women? Is this a system worth preserving?

I believe that both the rabbis and the women in talmudic times would have seen things differently had they known what we know now: that many women have short cycles and therefore ovulate before seven days after their bleeding stops. A woman's chances to conceive are limited to only about three to five days a month: the day (or two) before ovulation, the day of ovulation, and the day (or two) after ovulation. If women actually took this stricture upon themselves as a form of birth control in a time when birth was a life-threatening experience, then the reality has changed significantly enough in this area for this stricture to no longer apply. Today, with other forms of birth control, it would be absurd to keep this practice in place for this reason. Moreover, I have to assume the women did not think they were preventing themselves from ever conceiving, but rather saw themselves as limiting their chances.

As much as I try to understand these "daughters of Israel," I have to believe that their experience of menstruation and child birth was so different from mine that they were willing to push this rabbinic stricture so far. Or, I have to believe that this is simply untrue, that what is being recorded in the Talmud is not historical truth, but rather one version of what happened—a male version at that! Perhaps the women back then at most cooperated with the Rabbis (as a less well-known source on the next page, BT Nidah 67, suggests) but did not pro-actively take any strictures in this regard upon themselves (as BT Nidah 66 suggests).

And so, perhaps I could feel justified if I decided to stop keeping these seven clean days when what I was experiencing was surely *nidah*, normal menstruation. I could tell myself that both the Rabbis and the "daughters of Israel" had no idea their strict approach would limit the number of souls being brought into this world and cause the kind of suffering it does today. Since no Orthodox rabbinic authority today would be willing to stand up for "halakhically infertile" women, women today, like the women in medieval Egypt, would have to take this matter into our own hands.

> *Rabbi Yossi the Galilean expounded: When the Israelites*
> *emerged from the Red Sea after it split, the entire nation—even*
> *the infants lying upon their mothers' knees and feeding at their*
> *mothers' breasts—saw the Presence of God.*
> *According to Rabbi Meir, even fetuses in their mothers'*
> *wombs were able to see.*
> *Said Rabbi Tanhum, the wombs became as transparent as*
> *glass, and so even the fetuses were able to see the Presence of*
> *God.*
> — BT Sotah 30b-31a

It is no wonder to me that the fetuses in their mothers' wombs were able to see God's Presence after the splitting of the Red Sea. Having not yet been influenced by the human world, their connection to God would have been purely intuitive. The surprising thing was not that the fetuses could see the Presence of God, but that those who had already been residing in the human world for some time were still able to see the Divine Presence.

Today, we feel even more distanced from the Divine because no one can "see" the Presence of God. The age of splitting seas is long gone. Perhaps today we need to use a different sense—listening instead of seeing. The Bible tells us that each person was created in God's Image. Even after we are born into this world, a spark of the Divine remains within each and every one of us. The question is: How can we tap into that light inside ourselves? Perhaps, rather than looking towards something outside of ourselves, we must learn to listen to our own inner voice deep inside our soul and trust that it is reflecting our Divine Spark.

When I discovered that my periods were getting shorter, I went to visit my doctor to clarify with him that this was most likely causing my fertility problem. I left his office with a prescription for hormones that would delay my ovulation. But I never filled that prescription. I was horrified that this was my doctor's recommendation. While I knew that I could simply take these hormones and be free of my personal "problem," this was not just about me and my "problem." It was about male-dominated systems (both the medical system and the rabbinic system) dictating how women should treat their bodies. Moreover, I was not sick. I needed no medical treatment. And with a strong history of breast cancer in my family, I did not want to take hormones unnecessarily.

It became clear to me that it is the moral responsibility of all women to challenge a system that asks women to sacrifice their fertility, or their health, or their opportunity to conceive a child in the act of lovemaking, in order to preserve the patriarchal status quo. By treating ourselves like presumed *zavot*, we perpetuate this system. We allow contemporary rabbinic authorities to duck the question, rather than be courageous enough to implement a proper halakhic solution.

Suddenly, I felt strongly that it was time for all women to refuse to cooperate. By complying with this system, we were party to the crime of women's bodies being laid out on the altar in the name of Torah. This reality was there all along, but I simply could not see it. My vision had been clouded by years of complying with the system to prove that my motives in studying the halakhah were "pure" and not revolutionary.

When I stopped bleeding after my next period, on what happened to be seven days, I decided to treat myself as the *nidah* that, according to biblical law I was, and go to the mikveh. Although for the first few years of my marriage I had observed the ritual this way, for more than ten years now I had been practicing the seven extra "clean" days of separation. Habits are hard to break. Butterflies fluttered in my stomach as I walked over to the mikveh. But nervousness was only part of what this sensation was about. The other part was excitement. I felt like a new bride on her wedding night. A new chapter in my life was about to begin. I felt liberated. A little scared, a little unsettled. But free.

When I entered the mikveh building, a dilapidated, ugly institutional one-floor dump across the street from an empty lot, the mikveh attendant was asleep at the front desk. These women are overworked and underpaid, and they do this job out of a sense of mitzvah. Wouldn't the money be better spent on paying these women more and renovating this building rather than artificially inseminating healthy women and feed-

ing them hormones? The entire institution is an embarrassment—the
state of the building, the treatment of the mikveh attendants—a true *hil-
lul Hashem*, a desecration of God's name. The sleeping attendant looked
so peaceful I didn't want to wake her. Besides, I preferred to immerse in
private.

I took a towel, left my money on the desk, and went into one of the
rooms. The lock was broken, so I had to put a chair against the door to
keep it closed. I went through all of my regular preparations—washing,
scrubbing, combing—and entered the warm water. As I looked up at the
ceiling, I saw peeling paint and cobwebs, but I imagined myself alone
in a mountain lake beneath a starry sky. I felt totally at peace. I dunked
and said the blessing and dunked six more times—seven being a number
of wholeness and completion. Then I stayed in the water to sing and
meditate.

I of course prayed for a child as I immersed in the "living waters." But
this change in my practice felt much deeper than a simple temporary
measure to solve a particular problem. As I meditated in the mikveh
that night, I knew this was a change that would stick—irrespective of
my menstrual cycle and ovulation time, and irrespective of my personal
desire for a child. The reasons to return to the biblical laws of *nidah/zi-
vah* outweighed in my mind the arguments against such a move. Torah
must be just and good; if not, we are misinterpreting Torah. I could see
that now.

Moreover, having one week of non-sexual time and three weeks of
sexual time seemed like a more healthy approach to sexuality in marriage than there being a complete balance between the periods of time
when a couple can and cannot be sexual. After all, it's one thing to value
non-sexual time together, but it's another to make the sexual and non-
sexual time equal, thus normalizing what is actually not normal within
a healthy marriage.

God was returning me somehow to a deeper source that I had not
been able to tune into until now. A source that brought me closer to
God's Will and a purity that could never exist with all of the layers upon
layers of exclusively-male-interpreted Torah suffocating it. And while I
knew that I would never and could never tear myself completely from

those layers, I had to trust that there was a way to return to that original source, to tap into God's Will beneath all of those layers, to see it with my own eyes through the film that had been clouding my vision.

In order for me to live Torah in a truly authentic, passionate, and honest way, I had to feel one-hundred-percent at peace with this Torah. After all, no one could take responsibility for my choices but me. Not the author of the Shulkhan Aruch or any modern-day *nidah* manual, and not any *posek* of our time. Not the rabbi who taught me to examine the stains on my underwear to determine my *tumah* status. My religious decisions were my own, and I had to make sure they represented who I was in my very essence.

As I emerged from the mikveh I felt my vision had cleared. I thought of the midrash that told of the Israelite mothers' wombs that became translucent so that the fetuses they carried could see the Presence of God after the crossing of the Red Sea. I felt akin to those fetuses encased in their mothers' glass wombs. The tradition, the halakhah that male rabbis had been interpreting for centuries, had felt like opaque and impenetrable walls. On one hand, these walls provided a safe enclosure, but on the other hand, they suffocated. Now the walls of that safe enclosure seemed transparent. I still felt that they would protect me, nurture me. But I felt able to see through these traditions and laws, perhaps for the first time, to the Presence of God.

When I am trying to conceive, *tumah* becomes, for me, connected to death. Each time I menstruate when I want to be pregnant, I feel the loss of potential life. I can even begin to understand in a deep way how Rav may have associated *nidah* blood with death in the midrash about the Moabites. I see my womb as a cocoon in which life is germinated, and its lining is the membrane that protects the life within this cocoon. When the membrane flows out, not utilized, the potential to create life has gone untapped.

(It is not only menstrual *tumah* that is connected to death. A corpse is the ultimate source of *tumah*. And semen too causes *tumah*. Like the

uterine lining, semen represents life, but it can also represent the potential for life going untapped.)

The rabbinic institution of mikveh immersion is an especially welcome renewal ritual for me when I am trying to conceive. It gives me an
experiential way to renew my hope at the beginning of each new fertility
cycle.

When I am in *nidah*, when I am in this state of consciousness of being
teme'ah, there is a sense of mourning about me. I think I am more serious,
more contemplative, more internally directed, more aware of my own
mortality, of the finite nature of life. This one part of the month when I
am focused on mortality makes me more aware of it in general.

I was born with a degenerating muscular disorder, a form of muscular
dystrophy for which there is no cure. My condition has deteriorated in
recent years. And while it is not sharply debilitating, it does limit me in
ways of which I am constantly aware. *Tumah* (or mortality) consciousness is especially acute for me.

Having *tumah* in my life gives me a space in which to acknowledge
and appreciate this ultimate truth: I too shall die. My body is deteriorat-
ing before my very eyes. And there is nothing that I can do to prevent
this. I can live with this knowledge and make use of it to better my life,
but I cannot escape it any more than I can escape *tumah* itself. Like
death, when *tumah* comes, it comes. At least with *tumah*, I can wait it
out. There is an end in sight. Nevertheless, when I am *teme'ah*, I have to
live with *tumah*, inhabit it, be in it, and trust that in this state too there
is wisdom and truth.

If *tumah* is death, then *taharah*, purity, is life. When I come out of my
state of *tumah* by way of the living waters, I am renewed. Mikveh connects us back to the primeval waters, the waters of Creation that existed
before duality and mortality and the reality of living in an imperfect
world. Mikveh connects us back to our mother's womb, before we as
individuals entered this world and began our life-long striving for that
feeling of wholeness that we experienced floating in the amniotic fluid.
Our search for God, for spirituality, is for a way to reconnect to that
original source of life, that original experience of wholeness.

And so, when I am in the mikveh, I have that moment of reconnection—to that life-source and to my own spiritual center, which are, essentially, one and the same. Then, when I emerge from the mikveh, I feel reborn. I appreciate life as the gift that it is. Having been inside death, I am reborn into life with a fresh perspective. Life has that freshly washed look of trees after the first rain of winter in Jerusalem, when all of the dust from months of dry desert heat is washed away: filled with possibilities, with potential. Just as the womb becomes once again a potential site of creation, a potential life-giving, life-nurturing cocoon, the world and my individual life within it seem like a bud about to bloom, a seed about to sprout, a soul about to be born into what it was meant to be.

Living with death and life in this cyclical way is like living each month a microcosm of my life. And so, in this way, each month I am given the gift of a gentle tap on the shoulder, a subtle light flashing in my head, a reminder to truly live my life, to be present in my state of *taharah*, because I know that *tumah* is just around the corner.

I was three months pregnant when I was forced into a painful confrontation with the connection between *tumah* and the cycle of life. I was studying in a local co-ed yeshiva when the pain and heavy bleeding started. I went into the bathroom and did not emerge from the stall for two hours. The cramping—my uterus contracting in order to extricate this stagnant pregnancy—was so intense that I could not get up. I sat there on the toilet, rocking back and forth, trying to push out this fetus that I had so desired.

I mourned for what could have been, but I knew that there was no hope for this fetus. It had no chance to become a living, breathing being. Perhaps in that first month or so, it had. But somewhere along the way, probably around six weeks, it just stopped. I knew this because a month earlier the doctor had found no heartbeat. He had said that I could go straight to the hospital then and undergo a D&C procedure in which the uterus is scraped out, or I could wait to bleed naturally. I chose the latter route.

For over three weeks I waited, carrying a dead fetus. And in that waiting, in that place of the unknown, something happened to me. I had delved into the depths of my most inner self and faced some of my deepest fears.

Perhaps God had decided that this was the end of my childbearing years. Perhaps five was my limit. All of my children were born by Caesarean section—not an experience one can put her body through too many times. Plus, after the birth of my last child, I noticed that the muscular disease that had until then only affected certain of my facial and upper body muscles had progressed to certain muscles in my legs and feet as well. Walking required effort; I could only do so slowly and with a limp, and I tripped quite often. My body could not keep up with my dreams.

It was only then that I began to come to terms with the fact that this disease may disable me. Most likely, I would end up in a wheelchair rather than retiring to a life of hiking and biking. That notion had been difficult to face, and I had struggled with it intensely since Nachum's birth.

The miscarriage came in the midst of this internal struggle. I knew having this child was not a practical idea, not only because of my own physical condition, but also because there was a 50% chance that any of my children would inherit the disease. Thank God, it looked like only two of my children had; why press my luck? But I wanted another child, and it would be better to go through pregnancy and another C-section sooner rather than later, precisely because of my degenerating physical condition. Knowing this, the miscarriage put me in a vulnerable place. It was a drawn-out experience that spanned the course of almost a month—from the time I had my first worrisome ultrasound, to the second definitive one, to the time I actually began to bleed—and therefore left me much time for introspection and prayer.

In that month I discovered my fear of the unknown, of leaving this period of my life and moving on to the next phase; of the pressure of having to create a new identity for myself that did not include being the mother of young children, of having to fill the space that once had been filled with the day-to-day responsibilities that identity entailed. I also discovered my own deep sorrow. I did not want this period in my life to end. I loved my life as it was—its balance, its rhythm, its chaos.

As the month passed, I understood that this feeling of utter helplessness was meant to put me in a place of peace with whatever God had in store. I learned how to wait and trust. Enduring that month helped me realize that God is taking care of me, even if I cannot see the actual plan. I felt strongly the message that God was with me in this experience as much as in the births of my five children. By the time the actual miscarriage occurred, I was not in a place of shock or sorrow. I had mourned my loss. I knew I had to go through this in order to grow. I was letting the pregnancy go as I sat alone in a bathroom stall, unable to do anything but rock in pain.

After a while, I began to sweat profusely. I couldn't bear the heat. I needed to breath! I pulled off my shirt and pants and continued to rock in pain. When I felt like I might pass out, I knew that I had to get out of that bathroom. I had to get myself home. In spite of the pain, I put my clothes back on and emerged from the bathroom. On the way out, I caught a glimpse of myself in the mirror hanging over the sinks. I looked a ghostly shade of white-grayish-green, and I was covered in sweat.

Life was going on as usual out in the hall. Students were chatting, eating their lunches, laughing. I did not resent their levity. I wanted to get out of there unnoticed, but I could barely walk and did not make it to the door. I went right into the first open office door I saw and sat down next to a woman's desk. "I need to sit down," I said.

"I see. Of course," the woman said. "You look like you are about to pass out. Let me bring you some water," she said, her eyebrows furrowed. I could tell she was worried, but I was unable to get any words out to allay her concerns. So I just nodded. A few seconds later, she returned with a glass of water in hand. I drank. "Do you want to lie down?" she asked. "There's a futon in the office down the hall."

"No," I managed to say. "I want to get home. I'm miscarrying. I'm in a lot of pain."

"Can we help you get a cab? Someone can take you home."

At that point I realized I should call Jacob. Thank God he answered. I told him my predicament. "I'm in a lot of pain," I said. "I can't get home by myself. I can't even walk. Where are you?"

"It doesn't matter where I am. I'll come get you," he said, and hung up. I decided that it might be a good idea for me to make use of that futon while waiting for Jacob, so the woman lovingly walked me down the hall to an empty room where students can rest. "I'll give you your privacy," she said as she closed the door. How did she know that was the only thing I wanted besides the glass of water she came back with a minute later? God sends angels in many forms.

About fifteen minutes later, Jacob opened the door and walked in. He took one look at me and said: "Should we call the doctor? Maybe you need to go to the hospital."

"His number is in my phone book in my knapsack," I said.

Jacob called the doctor and told him how I was. He suggested taking pain killers and waiting it out. He said there was no need to go to the hospital unless I was hemorrhaging. Jacob drove me home. After some time with the pain still intense, Jacob called the doctor again. When he hung up the phone, Jacob said he was going out to the doctor's office to get a prescription for pills to hasten the contraction of my uterus. The pills would intensify the pain, but it would pass more quickly. Jacob went out to fill the prescription and left me lying in bed.

While Jacob was out, the pain suddenly stopped. The change was so abrupt that I felt like I was floating above my body—like my body had died, drowned, and I, my soul, was left floating above the surface of the water, in an absolute state of nirvana. I felt so at peace, and was so exhausted, that I fell asleep. When Jacob returned, I woke up. He handed me the pills. "He said to take them with a lot of water."

"I don't need them anymore," I said. "I'm okay now. The pain stopped. It's over. I feel totally fine." I felt better than fine. I felt like I could get up and go about my usual business. I could even go pick up the kids from school, which one of us would have to do in about fifteen minutes. But considering my condition, Jacob said he would pick up the kids and take them to story hour at the library, our usual Monday afternoon activity.

"Go back to sleep," Jacob insisted. "Rest some more."

I closed my eyes, but I could not sleep. I needed to cry. This was the first time I had cried since finding out that the pregnancy was not viable. After all the emotional pain I had been through the past few weeks and after all the physical pain of the past hours, it felt good to finally cry. Tears of release. I felt so drained, so empty, that it was like starting over with a fresh slate. There was still blood, but the worst was over. I was simply getting rid of what was left so that I could start a new cycle.

I still wanted to conceive again, but that was not what was most important now. I had learned these past weeks to stop the family planning. I had, thank God, five children—each one a world. My life was full of blessings and challenges. I would put myself in God's hands from now on.

Of course, that is what I had been doing all along. That is what we all do, especially when it comes to having children. And since Jacob and I had not used birth control since our first year of marriage, this had always been our approach in this area. Conceiving never came easily to us, and I had already had three miscarriages including this one, but thank God we were blessed with a relatively large family.

Nevertheless, I knew that I had never been able to totally give myself over to God in this realm of my life until now. I knew that from the jealousy I felt when I saw families larger than mine, when I saw pregnant women just when I was trying unsuccessfully to conceive, when I saw newborns suckling at their mother's breasts. I did not begrudge anyone their happiness. But when I wanted a baby, I wanted one so much that many benign things around me reminded me of that.

But lying there in bed, after what felt like a long and arduous journey—from a few days before Yom Kippur when I had the fateful ultrasound examination where the doctor found no heartbeat, through a week after Sukkot, when I miscarried—I felt that I finally truly put myself in God's hands. It felt as if a weight had been lifted from me. I felt lighter—as if I were being lifted up by the wave that is God.

I heard the door slam. Nachum walked into my room. I felt strangely as I did after my last four births, when the child who had been the baby only the day before walked into my hospital room. Nachum looked suddenly older, much bigger and more mature. But this time it was not because he looked so in comparison to a newborn. He looked older because I felt older. I felt more mature. This time, *I* had grown.

Nachum came over to my bed side, sippy-cup in hand. "I want to sleep with *Ima*," he said, climbing into my bed next to me. He pulled the blanket over his sneakered feet and up his jeaned legs and snuggled into me. I kissed his cheek and felt the cold from outside. Winter had begun. Only last week there was a *sharav*, a heat wave, and now it was winter in Jerusalem. The rain would fall so that things could grow, so that life could go on. I was content.

On the night seven days after the bleeding from my miscarriage stopped (a miscarriage this far into term, which is not a normal menstrual flow and usually lasts for longer than seven days, renders a woman a *zavah* according to biblical law, requiring her to wait seven clean days before she can immerse), I held a ritual gathering. Although this was my third miscarriage and not a novel experience, this miscarriage had been unique for me in that it had been such an intense growth experience; it felt important to ritualize the experience and to do so among a group of women. But, as when Michal got her period for the first time, I knew that the Jewish tradition offers no help in this area. No set and certainly no ancient ritual exists for women who miscarry, although individual women have created rituals to mark their own miscarriage experiences. And so, with no traditional precedents but much rich Jewish and feminist material to guide me, I created a ritual for myself.

I wanted my ritual to begin in the mikveh. Serendipitously, my mikveh night after my post-miscarriage bleeding fell out on *motzei Shabbat*, Saturday night, nine days after Rosh Chodesh. This was the night to recite *Kiddush Levanah*, the prayer sanctifying the New Moon—a prayer that seemed appropriate to incorporate into my ritual, since, about half a year earlier, I had taken upon myself the practice of reciting *Kiddush Levanah* each month, and since the main theme of this prayer is rebirth and renewal—the main themes I wanted my ritual to evoke. After all, this ritual was not about mourning my loss. I felt that I had gone through that already when I found out that the pregnancy was not viable. Rather, this was a ritual about my own rebirth and renewal as a result of this pivotal experience. I wanted to share my understanding that this pregnancy was not meant to grow a fetus. It was meant to grow me—to bring me through this experience to touch inner peace.

"You're ready to immerse," the elderly mikveh attendant told me in Hebrew. She was dressed in a long housecoat and all of her hair was pulled back into an opaque snood.

I slowly walked down the steps into the warm water, descending into the unknown. Trusting, waiting, floating, I was not afraid of the not knowing. I had learned to find holiness and peace in that wide open space. I dunked once, felt the waters envelope me like a hug. I stayed under for as long as I could, suspended yet totally immersed. With complete trust, I let myself go. Put myself into the hands of God.

I felt these waters protecting me. I felt only warmth and wetness. Nurturing and calming. Silence. Stillness. Total peace. Yet I could not stay too long. I had returned to the womb, only to be born again. I came up for air and recited the blessing:

"*Baruch atah Adonai Eloheinu melekh ha'olam, asher kidishanu bimitzvotav, vitzivanu al hatvilah.* Praised are You, Lord our God, Sovereign of the Universe, Who has sanctified us with Your mitzvot and commanded us regarding immersion."

Then I dunked again, and again, and again, and again, and again, and again. Seven times total, symbolizing the human spiritual realm. Seven is the Sabbath. The limit of Divine connection here on earth. I entered a dark tunnel, searched for my way out, and finally I reached the other end, the light. The light of seven. I tasted the World to Come. I touched the Divine here on earth. And now I was here to mark that encounter and transition back into the day-to-day reality of my life.

When I finished, the mikveh attendant wished me well. "May we hear good news from you," she said which I understood as a reference to my fertility. In other words, she was hoping not to see me again soon at the mikveh. She too wanted me to have another child. But I knew better now than to count on her blessings and well-wishes. I had been through that all too recently and intensely. I wanted to be left alone in my newly discovered space of peace. No hopes. No wishes. No expectations. Just total surrender.

I ascended the stairs and wrapped myself in the mikveh's scratchy

towel that the attendant held out for me. She left, closing the door behind her, yet leaving it slightly ajar. At last, I was alone. I decided to get
back into the water so I could relish the immersion as well as the transition out of the waters. My own rebirth. I sang aloud Psalm 118:23. A
friend had composed a niggun for me to the words of this psalm, which
I had chosen:

"Me'et Adonai haytah zot, hi niflat be'eineinu. This was from God. It was
wondrous in our eyes."

I concentrated on these words. This too was from God. This whole
experience, from the first portentous ultrasound to the excruciating day
of the miscarriage, from the moment I re-entered the womb to the experience of emerging into the light. God put me through this for a reason.
I was meant to change, to learn, to grow. And it was a wondrous journey
indeed! All of the blood and pain and tears. They were all from God.
They were sent to birth me.

I paid the mikveh attendant and walked out into the chill of autumn
in Jerusalem. Not cold enough to warrant a coat, but just enough nip
in the air to refresh and arouse. I hugged myself, rubbed my arms. The
fleece of my sweatshirt felt cozy and soft to the touch. It warmed me.
The smell of a wood-burning stove filled my nostrils. I hurried across
the street to my friend's house, worried that my friends may have been
waiting a long time.

The house was filled with the smell of popcorn and ginger when I entered. I had spent much of Friday morning baking, which was meant to
be part of my healing process. There was something nurturing in all that
repetitive motion: Measuring. Cutting. Combining. Separating. Mixing.
Pouring. Beating. Sprinkling. Shaping. First bran muffins, then corn-
bread, then ginger-pumpkin cake. One came out of the oven, the next
went in.

The baking was also meant to symbolize my state of mind, my willingness to trust, to take a leap of faith—as I had learned from baking
challah. You mix the ingredients, put the result in the oven, and hope
for the best.

Before Shabbat, I had brought the results of my bake-a-thon to my friend's house, so she could warm everything in the oven right after Shabbat. I wanted her house to be filled with these comforting aromas when my friends arrived. I also brought over the fixings for popcorn, another one of my comfort foods. I had spent many an evening (before kids) sitting in a movie theater—surrounded by people yet totally alone—watching one tear-jerker or another with the largest size of popcorn on my lap, crying. I loved going to movies alone.

What a luxury that would be for me now. The closest I've come to that in years has been renting a video at 11 at night when Jacob is traveling on business, after the kids are asleep. I've even made popcorn. But it's not the same. My kids are light sleepers. At least one or two will inevitably emerge, rubbing their eyes, perhaps even crying, and need to be given a drink or walked to the toilet, and then taken back to bed. That feeling of being totally alone cannot be replicated in my life right now, and might never be again.

But I didn't miss those days, at least not in the sense of feeling any regrets. They were good in their time. And this intense mothering stage was good in its time. And hopefully what was to come would be just as good, if not better. A combination of those days and these—independence without loneliness, space without emptiness—didn't sound so bad after all.

The women gathered around the coffee table in the living room. We sang the niggun. Again and again. *This was from God; it is wondrous in our eyes!* When the singing faded out, then stopped, I welcomed my guests. Looking around the room, I saw one face after another of amazing women, each of whom had been connected in some way to my recent experience. The rebirth of me. As I told my miscarriage story, I turned to one woman at a time, explaining how each woman present had helped and supported me.

Then I read a poem I composed for this occasion. The poem begins on Rosh Hashanah, a week before my first ultrasound, when we read in synagogue the story of Chanah praying for a child. She bargains with God, promises God that if she has a child, she will send him to work in the Tabernacle. So, when a son is born to her, after she weans him she sends him off. She keeps her promise to God. This son that she longed for and prayed so hard for, she dedicates to God. In the poem, I write about how, during that reading about Chanah on Rosh Hashanah, when I thought I was carrying a viable pregnancy, I was so upset by Chanah's willingness to give up her child that I closed my prayer book.

Then the poem moves to Yom Kippur, after the ultrasound, when I was waiting to miscarry. That Yom Kippur I felt so intensely the verse we sing repeatedly during the 25-hour fast: "We are like clay in the hands of the Creator." I prayed that Yom Kippur for guidance from Chanah, who only ten days before had made me close my prayer book in disbelief. Now I wanted to know her secret, to understand how she had the courage to surrender to God's Will. I wanted to learn from her how to grow from my pain, rather than wallow in it.

After I read the poem, I took out something I had been holding on to for some time: my pregnancy box. It contained three positive pregnancy tests; my ultrasound results; a time-line of my pregnancy provided by a new computer program for OBGYNs on my first pre-natal visit to the doctor; a prescription for folic acid and iron; and some referrals for further tests. It also contained a photograph my four-and-a-half-year-old daughter Hallel had cut out of a magazine a few days before: a picture of a beautiful blond woman with a smiling, content baby.

"This is you," Hallel had said as she handed me the picture. And I knew right away that this would go into the box, soon to be buried deep in the dirt of my small backyard. Despite a total lack of physical resemblance between me and the blond model in the photograph, that woman with her baby was me. It would always be me. But it was also not me. Or may not be me again. May be. Maybe not. But I was prepared to bury that part of my life if need be. Not buried and forgotten. But buried in my heart—a fond memory, but not a whole life, not the end of the story.

Now it was time for sharing. I invited my friends to tell their stories, share their thoughts. Each woman, after she spoke, drank pomegranate juice from my glass goblet, decorated with roses, the Miriam's Cup I use for the Passover seder at my house. Pomegranate juice, I explained, is what I drank when I felt ready to bleed. I knew this was what I needed. The idea stubbornly stuck in my head until I bought the juice and drank it warm to get those bloods flowing. Deep red liquid brings deep red liquid.

One woman spoke. She told of her own miscarriage at six months, what would have been her sixth child. She never did have any more children after that. She cried when she described the experience as "birthing death," and I wondered if my story would mirror hers. After all, this would have been my sixth child too. But this possibility did not sadden me. She looked perfectly content with her life. No regrets or disappointments. And I knew that if I were to have no more children, I would be as content as she was. She drank.

Another woman told about two successive still-births. She was sick, attacked by a deadly bacteria, and in order to save her life, they had to get her six-month-old fetus out of her. She tells us how she cried for weeks afterwards, both times, and how she did not want to return to the living. How she wanted to leave her three living children to be with this dead fetus. She cried all of the time, she says, until she made a conscious choice to live. And then the decision to try again, despite the risks to her life. And then, thank God, a baby girl. Her miracle baby. She drank.

Another woman told of her only son's birth. But none of us knew he had had a twin. This was the first time she had spoken of it to her friends. The twin fetus was lost when she was in the hospital, on bed rest. But she decided, then and there, to focus on *her* miracle baby and not dwell on what was lost. She drank.

Another woman, a mother of ten, said how her surrendering to God was all of those years of baby after baby, and that her decision to stop was her rebellion against God's Will. She still wondered where those souls she refused to bring into this world went. Perhaps into the bodies of her grandchildren or other children she has felt a deep connection to over the years? She drank.

After sharing, we went out into the clear, dark night to recite *Kiddush Levanah*—the prayer recited as the moon works towards its half-month fullness—together. This prayer is recited in a group, outside, with the moon in full view. We asked God to renew us like the moon is renewed each month. We leaped with arms outstretched to the moon, trying to reach it, touch it. We greeted one another, saying "*Shalom Aleichem*, peace be with you, *Aleichem Shalom*, with *you* be peace!"

I looked up at the almost-full moon. It had been ten days since Rosh Chodesh. Like the moon, I had been filled and emptied, emptied and filled. I prayed to be renewed like the moon, but by that I did not mean simply to be filled again with blood and the potential to conceive and birth another life. No, I meant a renewal of spirit, a rebirth of me. My womb was empty, and I too had been empty. But I could live in that empty space, and I could fill that empty space. And I could praise God for bringing me to a place where I could look up at the moon, marvel at its splendor, and truly be content in that moment.

I was surrounded by friends on a moon-lit night, praising God and our ability to be renewed, ready to go back to my home full of children and the man who I knew would love me and support my dreams whether we had ten children or none. And if he was still awake, we would be reunited in the closest way possible for two human beings to physically unite. And maybe, this time, our union would result in conception. And maybe it wouldn't. "Either way," my friend told me as she handed me a bottle of coffee liquor when the evening was over, "you'll have fun try-ing."

I felt I had reached a point where I was not "trying" anymore. As much as I wanted another child, I was open to whatever God had in store.

As I started to walk home, I realized that I still had one thing left to do. My plan was to bury my pregnancy box in my backyard, but as I walked past the empty lot across the street from the mikveh building on my way home, I knew that this is where the box belonged, near the "Living Waters."

It was a dark, chilly night. The moon was a sliver in the sky. I knelt down next to some overgrown bushes and began to dig with my bare hands. Dirt got caught in my fingernails, and my skin began to hurt from the rocky soil. But I kept digging. I felt such a need to get this done that I did not care about the discomfort. I did not shed a tear as I covered the box with stones and earth. The time was right. I was past this. I was headed down a path, and while I was not sure where this process would take me, I knew I was on my way towards birthing what was meant to come of this pregnancy. I was not there yet, but I felt God's hands guiding me, moving me forward.

As I buried the box, I heard in my head lines from *Shirat Hayam*, the song the Israelites sang as they crossed the Red Sea: "Deep waters covered them. They descended in the depths like stone...The mighty ones sank like lead in the waters." It was not the gruesome imagery of the Egyptians drowning that drew me to these verses, but rather, it was the sinking, the image of a stone or a block of lead falling deeper and deeper into the *tehom*, the depths.

I chanted these verses to myself as I walked home and imagined my box sinking as I walked. By the time I reached my house, I had a clear picture of this box, filled with my longings, resting peacefully on the ocean floor. And that was when another verse from *Shirat Hayam* came to me: "Who is like You among the heavenly powers, God? Who is like You, mighty in holiness, too awesome for praise, doing wonders!"

In synagogue on Shabbat, the week after my miscarriage ritual, I was struck, while listening to the words of the mourner's Kaddish, by how much it expressed one of the feelings I wanted to convey with my choice of *Kiddush Levanah* as part of my own ceremony. Much of *Kiddush Levanah* consists of praise of God, which is what came naturally to me after my miscarriage. I wanted to praise God for putting me through that difficult yet fruitful experience. I wanted to acknowledge my belief that even what may seem "bad" on the surface comes from God. It is all part of life, and we can grow from even painful experiences.

If I am to truly believe that God is protecting me when things are going well, then I have to believe that God is watching out for me as well when I am faced with difficulties and disappointments in my life. And so, I chose to praise God as part of my ritual. While I did not think about traditional mourning rituals when designing my own post-miscarriage ritual, it seems that many of my own personal needs for that ceremony match traditional Jewish practice in a case of actual mourning after death. This was especially interesting to me in terms of the connection between *tumah* and death.

Another example of this was my choice of a burial ritual. When I decided to bury my box of pregnancy-related items, I was not thinking about cemeteries or funerals, as strange as it may seem in retrospect. I was thinking of a way I could put the miscarriage behind me in a physical way. I needed to go through some kind of motion that would express my willingness to move on and accept the possibility that I may never give birth again.

Filling a tin box with items related to this pregnancy and my image of myself as the mother of another infant seemed like the right way to do it. But now, in retrospect, I see how burying the body of a loved one can also put some closure on the experience of their death. Their physical body is under the earth, out of sight. Perhaps not out of mind, but certainly no longer in the physical world, and therefore no longer part of what we could call our reality.

Another similarity I discovered was my counting of the seven clean days before immersing in the mikveh. Of course, that is the way we are told in the Bible to keep the laws of *zivah*, and so, it was not an intentional act of mourning on my part. Nevertheless, I did experience the mourner's counting of seven days of shiva after the funeral of a parent, spouse, or child.

Seven is a number of completion. I passed through a unit of time between the miscarriage—the "death"—and my ceremony, which, unlike a funeral, was less about mourning and more about renewal. My renewal. It was about coming out of the mourning period.

And there was the baking. After a death, the mourner is not supposed to prepare food; rather, the mourner is supposed to be taken care of by others. There is a strong tradition of friends and relatives bringing food for the mourner throughout the seven days of sitting shiva. The atmosphere in the shiva home should be one of comfort, which I wanted to create at my ceremony as well. But in my case, I wanted to provide that nurturing for both myself and those who came to comfort me, because I saw this ritual as being a catharsis not only for me, but hopefully for the other women present as well.

The last part of the ceremony was the sharing. Sitting in my friend's living room, offering our stories and thoughts, felt like the talk that often goes on at a shiva home, bringing the mourner into the community and not letting him or her mourn alone. Visitors to a house of mourning are told to simply come and sit, be a physical presence, even if the mourner does not want to talk. I too felt a need to bring my mourning out into the public. I did not want to mourn alone, which happens in the case of miscarriage.

It is fascinating how many people came to me to offer condolences after the ritual, even people I did not tell. Including men! The first two times, when they said, "I was so sorry to hear what happened," I had no idea what they were talking about, until they explained that they had heard about my miscarriage. Because I conducted a semi-public ritual, the news spread. While at first I may have been taken aback, in the end I was pleased that people were acknowledging my loss in this way. It felt right, comforting, even satisfying, as though this was part of the purpose of the ritual: to decrease the taboo surrounding discussion of miscarriage.

Why is miscarriage so secretive? Because, like early pregnancy, it is a sign of sexuality? Until a pregnancy is visible, people think it should be kept secret. Perhaps that is because the pregnancy may end in miscarriage. Twenty percent do. But that is a circular argument. Even if the pregnancy ends in miscarriage, why should a miscarriage be a secret?

Is it about superstition? The evil eye? Do we worry that by speaking of this misfortune, we may cause it to spread? If the miscarriage is not kept secret, there would be no reason to keep the pregnancy secret either. And vice versa. We could be open from beginning to end—whatever form that end takes. I know that would be a relief for me.

Perhaps because miscarriage is a liminal experience we keep it secret. It's not a death, but it is a loss of potential life. My fetus was not a life, but does that mean it was nothing? Meaningless? Are we hesitant to acknowledge the loss because by doing so we face uncomfortably deep questions about life and when it begins?

Or does the silence come from shame and guilt? Do women feel guilty when they miscarry, as if they have somehow brought this misfortune upon themselves? I thought our tradition discredited that kind of punishment theology of suffering with Job. But perhaps not.

When miscarriage is not acknowledged in any public way, the woman feels that her grief is unwarranted, silly, inappropriate. Having heard my women friends speak, I knew this was not so. In fact, most commended me on my ability to see the experience as positive, as a potential for growth, because this is something that they have not been able to do. Most of my women friends say that they never got over their miscarriages, unless they went on to conceive and give birth. And in many cases, they say that even after giving birth to a healthy baby, they still mourn the baby that never was.

I hope I have started a new trend with my post-miscarriage ritual, as well as with Michal's period party. In both cases, the impetus was personal, but a positive side-effect could be the slow lifting of the taboos around menstruation and miscarriage on a societal level. By creating and staging such public rituals, we positively reinterpret *tumah* as it relates to the blood that flows from our wombs and create positive associations and experiences connected to our uterine bleeding. We celebrate our reproductive power and the blood that makes it happen.

Has society been afraid to acknowledge women's reproductive power? Is that why there are no rituals to mark the onset of menstruation or the loss of a fetus? Ritualizing the onset of menses or miscarriage is totally and completely about the woman herself. It is about her body and its ability to bring life into this world. It is not about the birth of a baby, but it is about the woman's power and the power of her uterine blood.

Perhaps that is why this blood (and the woman from whom it flows) has, over centuries of interpretation and reinterpretation, been stigmatized as *tameh* on the one extreme, and ignored on the other extreme. If patriarchal society is afraid to deal with a woman's ability to bring life into the world—an ability so acutely represented by this blood—why should we women agree to be kept silent? Can we not reclaim our blood and celebrate it as the positive source of life that it is?

I am no longer going to be left to cry alone. And I am not going to let my daughters cower in shame at the sight of this blood. I am going to celebrate my blood and mourn my blood and do so among a community of women and then go out and share that celebration with the world, men and women alike. I will not hide.

The midrash[15] tells us that after Adam and Eve were expelled from the Garden of Eden, Adam immersed in the Gichon River, which flowed out from the Garden. Adam did this to repent for his sin of eating from the tree of knowledge. Perhaps he chose this specific river, with its direct connection back to Eden, because he was hoping God would remove his sin and return him to paradise. So he stood there with the water up to his neck for seven days, begging God to accept his repentance.

According to the author of this midrash, Eve was not the only one who sinned. Adam too was at fault. It is not only the women who need to make amends for the state of our imperfect world. It is not only women who need to immerse and be reborn. It is not only women who need to experience the cleansing, purifying, renewing feeling of total submersion in the living waters.

After seven days, God accepted Adam's repentance, but this did not mean sending him back to Eden. There was no turning back. Adam did not realize that the river's current flows in only one direction: out of Eden. He did not understand that each time we are reborn, we are born anew. We cannot go backwards. We can only go forwards. Water can purify, but it cannot erase what was. It can transform and transition and serve as a pathway into the future. But it cannot lead us back into the past.

A few months after my miscarriage ritual, I conceived again. But this pregnancy too ended in miscarriage. After two miscarriages in six months, I asked Jacob to do something I had wanted him to do since we were first married: immerse along with me before we resumed sexual relations.

After all, he was just as *tameh* as I was—not only from contracting my *tumah* (by sitting on the same chair I sat on, for instance), but also from

---

[15] *Pirkei D'Rabbi Eliezer*, chapter 20

other forms of *tumah*, even some of which originated in his own body, such as *tumah* contracted from seminal emissions. *Tumah* is a spiritual consciousness of the cycles of spiritual highs and lows, openness and closure, that we all experience in our lives. Is this "*tumah* consciousness" relevant to only women today? I think not. Men too can benefit from tapping into these spiritual rhythms.

For a variety of reasons (some technically halakhic and some ideologically misogynist in nature), post-Temple Jewish religious culture has channeled all of its *tumah* energy towards women, so that we have contained it more or less on our own since the destruction of the Temple. This has been both a blessing and a curse. Jewish women over the ages have been both uplifted and dragged down spiritually by this responsibility. The time had come for men and women alike to share in this experience, I decided. While I was well aware of the fact that the sexual prohibition attached to the *nidah* applies only to the woman's *tumah* status, the notion of us reuniting in a state of mutual *taharah* appealed to my longing for balance between me and Jacob in relation to this mitzvah, and for a more general balance between what has traditionally been called feminine, and what has traditionally been called masculine, spiritual experience in the world.

Moreover, when I immersed alone, it was difficult for me to turn my focus and intention away from my desires for another child. Since the last miscarriage, I *had* been focusing my thoughts on my marital relationship instead of my fertility issues while immersing—and this had been a powerful change for me—but after yet another miscarriage, I knew this would be more challenging. If Jacob were there with me, it would be different. His presence would help me shift the focus of my immersion from my own biology to something positive and enduring, something that went beyond my frustrations with pregnancy to mine and Jacob's everlasting love.

I was not looking to replace the ritual celebrating and marking my menstrual cycle. This was an important aspect of my immersion experience. Dunking beneath the living waters was precious to me. Yet, I was looking now to add a new dimension to my monthly immersions. I wanted this ritual to take on new meanings as I felt my life moving into a new phase.

Since the men's and women's mikvaot are separate and not open during the same times of day—the women's mikveh is open only at night, and the men's only during the day; and since a major reason for asking Jacob to immerse was that I wanted us to immerse together, our only option was to go to a natural spring, pool, river, lake, or to the ocean. So on the night of the seventh clean day after my blood flow stopped (I was clearly a *zavah* again in this case of a miscarriage that was certainly not a regular menstrual flow but also clearly not a birth), Jacob and I set out to Ein Halavan, literally, the "White Spring," which is about a twenty-minute drive from our home and has beautiful views of the surrounding Jerusalem hills.

At Ein Halavan the water comes from an underground source. There are two springs, one shallow and one deep. This is one of Jerusalem's answers to a watering hole, and people flock to this and other similar pools in the heat of summer. This was not the heat of summer, though. It was March, and while the days were warm, the nights were cold. When we arrived at Ein Halavan, towels in hand, it was dark. It was Rosh Chodesh Nisan, the beginning of the month the Israelites left Egypt, so there was only a sliver of a moon, but the stars were bright. They looked bigger than usual, giving the impression that we were closer to the heavens.

In the dark, we climbed a long flight of stone steps in order to reach the springs. I was still in a state of ritual impurity and therefore sexually off-limits, so we were still not touching. Therefore, we walked without holding hands, Jacob leading the way with a flashlight. When we reached the water's edge, my nostrils filled with a mossy, mucky smell. I looked into the pool. The water looked black, and I saw some leaves and branches floating on the surface.

"I wonder how cold it is," I said.

"Put your hand in."

I put my hand in. It was cold. I removed my fleece sweatshirt, my foam shoes, and my sweatpants. I wasn't wearing undergarments. I had the foresight to leave those at home, knowing that in the dark it was best to keep this as simple as possible.

Once undressed, I sat on the edge of a rock with my feet in the water.

"Okay," I said. "Are you watching? You have to make sure I go completely under." Then I jumped, swam out into the center of the pool, and dunked my whole body beneath the water. It wasn't freezing, but it was quite cold, so I decided to forego my custom of dunking seven times. I swam back to the rocks and pulled myself out of the water. Once I had a towel around me, I recited the blessing.

"Okay. It's your turn now," I said.

"How cold was it?"

"Not so bad. Really."

"But you're a water person. You don't mind this. You like it. I, on the other hand—"

"Go ahead."

Jacob came to where I was standing on a stone ledge by the water, and he removed his sweatshirt, slip-on shoes, underwear, and jeans. "The things I do for you," he said as he jumped. Then he yelped, "It's freezing!" and dunked under the water.

As I watched Jacob immerse, I thought of Adam up to his neck in water. The Rabbis created Eve as our model of atonement for the world's imperfections—we were given the *nidah* ritual as a means to atone for Eve's having caused Adam's death, the midrash tells us—but they also created a parallel model in Adam, it seems. I felt that the time was ripe to give Adam his fair chance at mikveh.

This felt to me now like a way to repair the damage that had been perpetuated throughout the years that *tumah*-related rituals, aside from *nidah*, fell into disuse, and only women became associated with *tumah*. By insisting that men immerse too before a couple can sexually reunite, it becomes a ritual about the couple's purification for each other, and the renewing of their sexual relationship.

And on a higher, cosmic level, mikveh immersion can be a ritual about mutual atonement, and a step together, in cooperation, towards repairing our broken world. By bringing Jacob into this ritual in a practical, tangible way, we performed a *tikkun*, a corrective, on the gender imbalance that exists in so many ways in our society. The more men and women invade and join together in each other's spaces, the better our society will become.

When Jacob pulled himself out of the water and was back at my side, I handed him a towel. Once it was wrapped around him, he kissed me hard on the lips. We hadn't touched for three weeks, since the bleeding from the miscarriage lasted for two weeks, and then I had to count seven clean days, as per the instructions for a *zavah* in Leviticus. It was nice to feel his smooth, wet lips on mine again. I kissed back. We opened our mouths, explored with our tongues. Jacob wrapped his towel around the both of us, and between the extra towel and the body heat, I was already warm. Jacob, on the other hand, was not.

"You're shivering," I said.

"It was so cold." Another kiss. "I'm still suffering the after-effects." Tongue exploring in my mouth again. "But now I'm beginning to warm up." He pulled me closer to him, skin against skin. "This part I like. I could do without the mikveh part, but this makes up for it."

Before we knew it, we were making love on the cold rocks on the side of the dark pool beneath a starry sky. After almost sixteen years of marriage, we still excited each other—something we already knew. But skinny-dipping on a chilly night under the stars certainly increased the fun and the passion. As did the aura of secrecy (almost naughtiness) that came with sneaking out of the house at night to do something as alive as this.

I thought of the cars we saw parked in the lot at the bottom of the steps—clearly other couples who had come to this secluded spot for some lovemaking of their own. None were as crazy as we were—the night was chilly for skinny dipping—but romance was in the air.

If we had thought of bringing a blanket and didn't have five children waiting for us at home, we could have stayed out there all night, lying in each other's arms, gazing at the awesome sky. But we had no blanket, and we did have five kids at home, with the oldest, 12-year-old Michal, in charge. So we dressed and walked back to the car—this time, hand-in-hand.

Before this night, I had felt exclusive responsibility for this mitzvah and our family planning, as I checked and counted and went off to the mikveh alone. But after Jacob and I emerged from the water, I felt empowered to face the unknown, because I knew we were in this together. I was reminded of the midrash in which all of the Israelites—infants and seniors alike—emerge from the Red Sea equally facing the mighty Presence of God. What God had in store for me was a mystery, but I could face it as long as my partner's hand was in mine. No matter what, I was not in this alone.

"Well, that wasn't so bad," Jacob said, as he wrapped me in an embrace. "I know I'll be looking forward to coming here again next month."

I too would be looking forward to coming here next month, and for many more months in the future. It was hard for me to believe that I had been going to an indoor institutional mikveh, alone, for all these years. This felt so clearly the way this ritual should be performed. I don't want to say this is how it *was meant* to be performed, because I am sure this is not what the Rabbis intended: husband and wife skinny dipping on mikveh night. But in our paradigm, this felt like the most appropriate way to carry out this ancient mitzvah.

I became able to see a meaningful future for me in relation to this mitzvah. A future without childbirth wasn't so bad after all. Outings like this one would be easier with no babies at home. It would be like returning to our dating and honeymoon days.

"So you'd do this again, mikveh and all?" I asked him, wondering if Jacob felt akin to Adam immersing in the Gichon. It's not as if I imagined he could ever feel compelled to stand up to his neck in water for seven days, but the fact that he mentioned coming here again next month convinced me that he was beginning to feel connected to this mitzvah.

"Mikveh and all," was his answer.

The Gemara[16] interprets the opening verse of the Book of Ruth: "*Vayihi biyimei shfot hashoftim,* And it was in the days when the judges judged," as follows: *Dor sheshofet et shoftav,* it was a generation that judged its own judges.

Rashi, Rabbi Shlomo Yitchaki, the famous medieval French Talmud scholar, adds that the judges themselves were corrupt. In other words,

---

[16] BT Baba Batra 15b

when those in power are corrupt or, in our view, are not correctly interpreting the word of God, it is our responsibility to critique them, to set them straight.

This is a huge responsibility, and often an uphill battle. How can one fight the system? How can one struggle against those in power? The best way to start is by refusing to cooperate. Then, even if the voices of protest are not heard, at least those who dare to protest have saved their own souls.

Spring is upon us, and Jacob and I are at the wedding of our friends' daughter. I should be crying as this couple stands beneath the chuppah, the marriage canopy. After all, I cry at most weddings, and this one is certainly an emotional one. The bride's parents are good friends of ours, and I am happy for them and for the couple. Yet, rather than cry, I grow more anxious and upset as the ceremony goes on. The bride, a quiet soul, internally directed, does not say a word. She is totally passive. The groom, on the other hand, places the ring on the bride's finger and recites the line, "*harei at mikudeshet li bitabaat zu,* You are hereby sanctified to me with this ring." With that act, he acquires her and declares her forbidden to all other men.

Two people becoming sanctified to each other is a beautiful occurrence. This, in fact, is what being married is about: Making a relationship holy. But this is not what this ceremony is about, because this is not a reciprocal act of sanctification. It is the woman who is sanctified to the man, giving herself to him. She will be sexually permitted only to him, whereas by biblical law, the man can have sex with, even marry, as many women as he can afford to support. The legal act is not mutual.

In other words, what is actually taking place in terms of the Jewish legal reality is the binding of the woman to the man forever, unless he should choose to set her free. He performs a ceremonial act of acquisition, similar to how, in Jewish Law, one undertakes to possess an object, an animal, or a piece of property. The man was never "sanctified" to the woman.

Of course, the woman has more rights in the relationship than a camel does. She has conjugal rights, and the husband is required to support her; even if he divorces her (as long as the divorce was not due to her rebellion), he is required to pay her a sum of money so she is not left destitute. The act of acquisition that takes place during a traditional Jewish marriage is unique in Jewish law. And there are blessings recited at the ceremony as well. There is clearly more than the purchase of a woman going on beneath the chuppah. Yet, it is impossible to get around the fact that acquisition is the legal model for Jewish marriage.

At past weddings, this legal reality did not bother me so much. It's not that I was unaware of the meaning and ramifications of the ceremony. At my own wedding, Jacob and I insisted on inserting whatever gestures the rabbi who married us would allow in order to make the ceremony seem more egalitarian.

But the rabbi did not allow much. He would not even allow me to give Jacob a ring under the chuppah; so I gave it to him in private after the ceremony was over. Even so, Jacob's childhood friends from the modern Orthodox community in which we grew up teased him for agreeing to wear a wedding ring at all.

In addition, Jacob signed a pre-nuptial agreement, in which he agreed to pay a specified amount of money each month should he ever refuse to give me a *get*, a Jewish writ of divorce, since it is the man alone who has the power to end the marriage. I also gave Jacob a "marriage statement," in which I wrote what I considered my responsibilities to him in marriage, to act as a balance for the traditional *ketubah* he signed and gave to me. The rabbi would not let me read this statement aloud under the chuppah. But I did read my statement aloud at the reception, and I introduced it by explaining how our marriage would be an egalitarian one, despite the power relationship set up by the ceremony we had just participated in an hour before.

These were all acts of resistance. But they were symbolic. In reality, Jacob and I had acquiesced to the system. He had acquired me, and I had allowed myself to be acquired. No matter how egalitarian our intentions were, from that point onwards, Jacob wielded the same theoretical power over me that all men married in a traditional Jewish ceremony wield over their wives: the power to withhold a divorce unless their wives comply with their every demand.

Now, standing at my friends' daughter's wedding sixteen years later, I feel that whatever amount of reinterpretation Jacob and I succeeded in accomplishing at our wedding was not enough. After jumping together with Jacob into that cold natural spring a few months before, I came to realize that the traditional marriage ceremony that Jacob and I staged did not reflect the nature of our relationship. The feeling of mutuality I felt when Jacob and I emerged together from those transforming living waters gave me new insight into the direction in which we need to be headed to reach a Judaism that is more healthy and balanced. And so, by the time my friends' daughter's wedding was over, I decided to take a course on the Jewish laws of marriage and divorce at a local women's yeshiva.

In Israel, all Jewish marriages and divorces are processed by the Israeli government rabbinate. Therefore, all such marriages and divorces are performed according to traditional Jewish law.

According to biblical law, a woman may have only one husband, but a man may have more than one wife. Also due to the unilateral nature of rabbinic marriage, it is only the man who can effect a divorce. He must write a writ of divorce, a *get*, for the woman and give it to her in front of a *beit din* of three legal witnesses. The woman can never do this herself, and even the *beit din* cannot do this without the man's willing consent.

Later, in 1040 C.E., Rabbeinu Gershom issued two important edicts that advanced the rights of women in Jewish marriage and divorce. The first outlawed polygamy among Ashkenazic (Eastern European) Jews, although no such edict was issued regarding Sephardic and Oriental Jews. The second declared that the woman must accept the *get* willingly. Before these edicts, a man could have many wives and divorce them without their consent.

Despite Rabbeinu Gershom's edicts, it is still only the man who can give the *get*, and he must do so willingly. No matter what sanctions the judges place on the man, they cannot force the *get*. Therefore, the man can always wield his power over the woman and blackmail her for whatever divorce arrangement he wants before he will give her the *get*; or he may refuse to give her the *get* under any circumstances. There are men who prefer sitting in Israeli jails to giving their wives a *get*.

The woman can also refuse to accept the *get*. However, it is only by rabbinic and not biblical law that the woman must agree to the divorce. Therefore, the man may enlist one hundred rabbis to waive the edict of Rabbeinu Gershom in his case by convincing them that the woman is being unreasonable and consequently her agreement is not needed.

What this means practically is that built into the traditional Jewish marriage and divorce system, and therefore the marriage and divorce system of the State of Israel, is every man's right to blackmail his wife until she agrees to his terms before he will grant a divorce. In fact, the lawyers and judges in the religious courts encourage men to do this.

The course I attended was designed to train people to spread the word about pre-nuptial agreements as a way to push for change in the system. These pre-nuptial agreements, like the one Jacob signed before our wedding, obligate the man to pay a specified amount as long as he withholds the *get*. The particular pre-nuptial agreement promoted by the organizers of this course is a mutual one; it is signed by both the man and the woman and obligates whichever partner is holding up the divorce to pay a monthly sum, so that if the wife is the one delaying the divorce, she will be the one to pay.

I took the course to learn the ins and outs of pre-nuptial agreements so that I could educate couples and encourage them to sign one. I came out of the course, however, more radical in my thinking than when I went in. I became convinced that pre-nuptial agreements are at best a last resort for couples who absolutely insist on the traditional one-sided ceremony. They are only a band-aid; maybe they will heal the wound or protect it—but they do not get to the root of what is causing the wound in the first place.

The first lecture in the series depressed me. The rabbi presented one horrible halakhic ruling after another: men who beat their wives, one man who even shot at his wife—and the *poskim*, the halakhic authorities, declared that they couldn't force the husbands to give their wives a *get*. The presenting rabbi argued the hands of the *poskim* were tied—or at least they felt this was the case. They stated they had no choice because if the *get* was not given willingly by the man, the *get* would not be a kosher *get*, and the woman would not be halakhically divorced.

These authorities claimed to fear bringing *mamzeirim* (children born from a forbidden sexual union, i.e. a married woman and any man besides her husband) into the world should these women go on with their lives, remarry, and have children without a *get* that is 100% unarguably kosher. If it should come out that this *get* is not kosher, that it was not given willingly by the husband, the children of her new marriage would be *mamzeirim*, and *mamzeirim* can only marry other *mamzeirim*.

I did not accept this argument. *Mamzeirim* were not the issue, because if the rabbinic authorities of our time wanted to write out the category of *mamzer* from our current halakhic reality, they could do so.[17] The Rabbis in the Talmud effectively eliminated the category of *ben sorer umoreh*, the biblical rebellious son, who must be put to death. They could declare everyone today a *safek mamzer*, a presumed *mamzer* (like they declared all women bleeding from their uterus *safek zavot*), and that would make everyone free to marry. Or they could find a way to narrow down this status in such a way that it would not apply to anyone today, as was done with *ben sorer umoreh*. But they would only do so if they felt the *mamzer* was actually an irrelevant or unethical label. Or *poskim* could change the nature of Jewish marriage ceremonies all together. They could remove the one-sided acquisition and thus equalize the marriage ceremony. Therefore the divorce process would become egalitarian as well.

Orthodox rabbinic authorities do not seek either of these approaches. Rather, they preserve the existing power structure within traditional halakhic Jewish marriage. In my opinion, their fear of *mamzeirim* is actually a fear of free women, women who are not under the control of

---

[17] In fact, some modern *poskim* have attempted to do so by declaring that if the woman claims "*mais alai*" (living with this man is unbearable to me) this is enough from a halakhic point of view so that the children of such a woman's union with another man, even if her husband never gives her a *get*, are not considered *mamzeirim*. Nevertheless, if this approach is not accepted by the majority of *poskim*, it will not make a difference in the Israeli religious courts.

anyone but themselves, their own moral conscience. As one prominent
medieval halakhic authority, the Ro"sh, Rabbeinu Asher, writes: "If a
woman could extract herself from under her husband's rule, no woman would remain under her husband, but rather they would all betray
their husbands and go off with other men."[18] It seems that the fear of
"*mamzeirim*" is really a fear of wanton women—of women's unbridled
sexuality. If the rabbinic authorities of our generation recognized this
view as the affront to God's name that it is, if they saw that women are
made to suffer unjustly in the name of God—or, more accurately, men's
interpretation of the Word of God—they might then change the status
quo.

Even *poskim* who recognize the injustice claim that their hands are
tied. For instance, the early 20th century halakhic authority Rabbi
Eliezer Waldenberg, author of the book of halakhic responsa Tzitz
Eliezer, seems to recognize the injustice in these cases. That is why he
suggests that the rabbinic courts require a recalcitrant husband to fully
support his wife even if he and she are no longer living together. Rabbi
Waldenberg's thinking is that hopefully the husband would realize that
it would be financially beneficial for him to divorce his wife rather than
support her for the rest of her life.

However, Rabbi Waldenberg also recognizes that this, like signing a
pre-nuptial agreement, is not really a "solution." A man who can't even
afford to support his wife at all, or a man who is so wealthy that sup-
porting her will not be a problem for him, could keep his wife in chains
indefinitely. And a man who is crazy or vengeful enough to even sit in
jail rather than divorce his wife would also withstand this law. What of
women whose husbands are in a coma or have disappeared altogether?
They too would remain in limbo.

The Tashbetz, Shimon bar Tzemah Doron, in 14th-15th century Al-
giers, does offer an actual solution. He writes that if a man is making his
wife's life miserable, the rabbinic authorities can force him to give her a
get. He cites the Talmud's ruling that in the case of a bad smelling man,
the *get* can be forced. Does it not seem logical, he concludes, that in a

---

[18] *Shut HaRo"sh* 43:8

more extreme case, the *get* can also be forced?!"[19]

This approach seems the most humane and the most reasonable, but it is not accepted by mainstream halakhic authorities. They claim their hands are tied by the halakhic requirement that the *get* be given 100% willingly by the man. But as the interpreters of halakhah, they are the ones tying their own hands. In other words, if the *posek* does not want to change the status quo, it is because the *posek* sees some value in retaining the current reality. Even if the *posek* recognizes injustice in the current system, he may feel that the loss in overturning the status quo will be too great, and opt for no change. This is still a choice.

We are told in the Bible: "Justice, justice you shall pursue!" If we see injustice, especially in our own religious system, we have the responsibility to find a way to interpret the halakhah so that there is justice. In fact, the concept of tikkun olam (repairing the world) originates in the Mishna in the very context of correcting problems created by Jewish Law itself, including issues of divorce. If halakhah is not just, it can't be God's Will. Permitting injustice in the name of God is a huge affront to God's name!

The rabbi presenting this session did not attack these rulings. He presented them with sympathy. I knew he was active in the struggle to find a halakhic solution to what he at least recognized as a problem, and his task that night was to make us see that there is indeed a problem. But what unsettled me about his presentation was that he did not present these rulings as unjust; rather, he presented them as acceptable halakhic rulings under the circumstances. He conveyed that the rabbis who wrote these rulings actually recognized the injustice in their own rulings but felt powerless to fix the situation.

He favored implementing prenuptial agreements. He felt that if couples sign these agreements, it would limit the number of such cases to only those few where the husband was cruel or crazy or ill or not present. But the *poskim* had written these unacceptable (in my eyes) rulings specifically in such cases! The rulings were in response to abuse, even attempted murder! In such cases, the prenuptial agreement would probably not work.

---

[19] *Shu"t Tashbetz* 2:8

The Talmud hints at a solution: A court can use its power to retroactively nullify the act of acquisition that solemnized the marriage. The Conservative movement instituted *kiddushin al tenai* as their mode of marriage, which means that all marriages performed in the Conservative movement are conditional on the man not withholding a *get* from his wife if she asks for one. In addition, Rabbi Emanuel Rackman, a Modern Orthodox rabbinic leader who died in 2008, led a valiant effort to create a *beit din* (rabbinic court) that took the unilateral power out of the hands of the man and put it in the hands of the *beit din*, empowering the *beit din* to dissolve marriages on the claim that the woman would never have agreed to marry this man in the first place had she known he would keep her in chains; according to this approach, such a marriage was never valid.

Rabbi Rackman was demonized by his modern Orthodox peers for this, and his *beit din* was rejected. Moreover, his approach and that of the Conservative movement (also rejected by the Orthodox) retain the unilateral acquisition, which preserves inequality in the Jewish marital relationship. Even a conditional marriage retains the basic power structure in which the man is the only active side in the transaction that takes place beneath the chuppah. As long as this hierarchical structure is preserved, even if only in theory, we have not created a ceremony that truly sanctifies the marital relationship.

Inequity in traditional Jewish marriage must be rejected. The best solution, I realized after sitting in that course for two months, was to get rid of acquisition in marriage all together. There is no reason to use a one-sided model for the Jewish marriage ceremony anymore. Why would we want to promote a model of marriage based on a commercial transaction? No reinterpretation can be convincing enough to present the acquisition of a woman as a holy act. Other, more suitable models that represent a holy marriage should be implemented.

Rachel Adler, the once-Orthodox-feminist-now-Reform-theologian, has done much work in this area. Inventing a new term for Jewish marriage, "*brit ahuvim*," a covenant of lovers, she chooses the halakhic category of *shutafut*, partnership, as the appropriate model for a marriage. A partnership is a relationship formed by a mutual agreement that the partners can enter into and dissolve at will.

I endorse the *brit ahuvim*, in which couples write a partnership agreement that lays out the terms of their relationship, as well as what they see as their joint responsibilities to their greater community and the world in general. But this should only be one aspect of the wedding. I would add another legal model to elicit the holiness of marriage. Both man and woman could take a vow to be monogamous. To break this vow, the couple would have to assemble a *beit din* of three. Therefore, this would prevent divorce from becoming a light matter.

I walked out of the course on prenuptial agreements seeing them as a last resort for a couple insisting on the traditional marriage, the only legal option in Israel. But I would strongly advise them not to marry through the official Israeli rabbinate.

For my own children, I was quite clear that I did not want them to marry through the rabbinate, but rather marry with a ceremony that truly reflects the way they view their marital relationship. This is a stand against the State, since the government would not recognize their marriage (unless it was also solemnized by a government official in a foreign country, such as Cypress). It would be an act of civil disobedience necessary to challenge this unjust system.

And if the worry of contemporary rabbinic authorities is that the entire edifice of Torah will collapse if men do not reign supreme, we will have to prove them wrong. We—men and women alike, with hands joined—must take the power away from these rabbis and claim it for ourselves. If these authorities prioritize protecting their own power, we cannot rely on them to mete out justice. Nor can we let our own desire for power, or for acceptance by those in power, impede our decision-making process. We have a responsibility to do things differently, to make sure justice and halakhah answer to each other.

The medieval commentator on the Gemara, Tosafot HaRosh, writes: "If the court ruled and one of its members, or a student worthy of ruling, knew they had erred… he is liable, because he was not dependent on the court."[20] In other words, when an individual sees that a *beit din* is acting unjustly, it is his or her responsibility to act against it.

---

[20] BT Horayot 2a

I am standing once again beneath the chuppah with Jacob at my side. We are at Kibbutz Ketura surrounded by our children and a small group of close friends. We came to the kibbutz to celebrate the holiday of Shavuot, when the Israelite nation received the Torah at Mt. Sinai. But since it is also our 18th wedding anniversary, we decided to celebrate that as well by renewing our vows. Doing so right after the holiday of Shavuot seemed especially appropriate, because Revelation at Sinai is often compared to a wedding in rabbinic literature. The mountain is depicted as a chuppah and the groom and bride are God and the Jewish People. In both cases, a covenantal relationship is being initiated and cemented.

Kibbutz Ketura is located in the middle of the Negev desert, so we are surrounded by stark mountains beneath a star-studded sky. The setting evokes what the desert scene at Mt. Sinai must have been like those thousands of years ago. The air is cooling off, although the day was quite warm down here in the southern part of the country. Jacob puts his arm around me, and I reciprocate the gesture as we listen to our friends and family clap and sing excitedly in Hebrew the traditional Jewish wedding song: "Soon we will hear in the cities of Judah and in the outskirts of Jerusalem: the voice of elation, the voice of joy, the voice of the groom and the voice of the bride."

Our chuppah is made of my tallit and Jacob's tied together, while the chuppah at our first wedding ceremony was only Jacob's tallit tied to four wooden poles. Jacob and I are both wearing white, as we did 18 years ago, but this time I am not in a wedding dress. My wedding garb this time is a *kittel*, a white cotton robe worn (usually) by Jewish men at certain ritual occasions, as is Jacob's. I do not look like a delicate china doll ready to be purchased and placed on a shelf. And facing us is a close woman rabbi friend who lives at the kibbutz. She will officiate at our ceremony this time, and unlike the Orthodox rabbi who officiated at our first ceremony, she is following the ceremony we chose for this occasion instead of the other way around.

After I completed the course in Jewish marriage and divorce, I reread an article I had read years before by Rabbi Meir Feldblum, who was a professor of Talmud at Yeshiva University and Bar Ilan University; in the article[21], Feldblum claims that most traditional Jewish marriages today are not valid, since the parties do not have the proper intention needed to effect the acquisition. The groom has no intention of acquiring his wife and wielding that power over her, and the bride has no intention of being acquired and putting herself under her husband's reign—even if she loves and trusts him as they stand, starry-eyed, beneath the chuppah.

With this in mind, it became important to me that Jacob and I conduct a *valid* marriage ceremony, because we would be aware and present under the chuppah this time around. The first time, we were united in our intention to commit to living the rest of our lives together in a mutually supportive and monogamous relationship, but in reality, the ceremony we underwent placed us in an unequal power relationship and limited my sexuality much more seriously than it did Jacob's.

Feldblum presents an alternative for the modern wedding ceremony: *derech kiddushin*. This option looks like the traditional act of acquisition, the *kiddushin*, but is not actual *kiddushin* because it lacks the unilateral *kinyan*. *Derech kiddushin* has Talmudic roots and is a way to sanctify and permit cohabitation without requiring a *get*.[22] This is the model Jacob and I therefore decided to adopt for our second ceremony.

And so, this time, when Jacob hands me my wedding ring, he says: "*Harei ani miyuchad lach bitabaat zu*, Behold I am made exclusively yours with this ring."

---

[21] "*Ba'ayot Agunot uMamzerim*," in *Dinei Yisra'el*, XIX (5757-5758).

[22] The core case of Feldblum's argument comes from a discussion of the status of a minor female whose father traveled abroad and thus effectively abandoned his obligations to his daughter–a father can contract marriage on behalf of his daughter, but a minor female cannot contract her own marriage (this was intended to protect her from sexual predators). In a case where such a girl attempts to take her fate in her own hands, the Rosh, in Kiddushin 2:8, asserts that though she cannot contract a kosher marriage on her own (she's still too young), "nevertheless, she cannot be forbidden [such a relationship] because she is to be considered an unmarried girl who engages in a licentious relationship [with her consort] for, since she is with him in the manner of marriage (*derech kiddushin hi ezlo*), it is not licentiousness." The relationship isn't full Rabbinic marriage because the partners weren't technically eligible to marry, but it's not licentiousness either—it doesn't require a *get*, but it's something more than concubinage. This, then, is *derech kiddushin*. (This position is mentioned in the *Shulkhan Aruch*, Even ha-Ezer 37:14.)

R. Feldblum suggests that any relationship that's in "the manner of marriage," even if it's not actually 100% fully kosher *kiddushin*, is sanctified yet does not require a *get*.

Then I hand him his wedding ring and say: "*Harei ani miyichedet lichah bitabaat zu*, Behold I am made exclusively yours with this ring."

Then we each take an official *neder*, a vow, of monogamy: "*Konam alei hanaat tashmishan shel kulam chutz mimech/mimchah kol zman sheanu miyuchadim echad lasheini*, The pleasure of intercourse with anyone except you shall be forbidden to me as long as we are exclusively each other's."

Then we read aloud the *shutafut* partnership document that we composed together. The reading of this document is followed by the traditional reading of the *Sheva Brachot*, the seven wedding blessings, and the breaking of the glass (this time, we have two glasses, one for me and one for Jacob), which, we explain, symbolizes the destruction of Jerusalem and the kabbalistic "breaking of the vessels," which should remind us of the tremendous amount of work that has yet to be done in this world.

As I put my foot down hard on the glass and hear it shatter, I am reminded again of the fetuses encased in their mother's glass wombs, and how they were able to see God's presence from that warm, wet, secure place. My marriage with Jacob has always felt like a womb for me—nurturing in a way that is not stifling but rather liberating. And now that we have sanctified our marriage further with a ceremony that reflects its true nature, I feel that we have raised the level of holiness one notch higher so that the bloody uterine walls have turned to crystal-clear glass before our eyes.

As we stand beneath the chuppah on equal footing, we not only sanctify our own relationship, but we bring God into the picture. With this change, we have come closer to what I believe God wants for this world: justice, love, and compassion. Each human being is equal in the eyes of God and should therefore be equal too in this most sacred of moments beneath the chuppah. And thus, we emerge from beneath the chuppah this time as we did that night from the "Living Waters," as the Israelites did centuries ago from the Red Sea: clearly able to see the presence of God.

Our second wedding could be seen as a shattering of sorts. As we each shattered our glass beneath the chuppah, this ceremony and hopefully more like it for other couples in the future will shatter the hierarchical gender relationships that are the root of so much injustice that is meted out in this world in the name of Torah. Our task is to put the shards back together—not to recreate the past, but rather to create a future that is connected to that past yet also reconfigured and fresh.

As Adam stood neck-deep in the water, we must put ourselves in this scary, vulnerable place before God, and hope for the best. Hope for God's Hand to reach down and help us put the pieces in the right places. But this will only push us into the future. We cannot return to Eden, but we can try to create a world that is like Eden was and even better, because it will be built upon the painful lessons we have learned about power and hierarchy and gender relationships that can never be truly holy as long as they are imbalanced.

Yes, in Eden we lived in bliss, but that was because we did not have the knowledge that we have today. No. There is no turning back. And why would we want to?

FIRE

HADLAKAT HA-NER:
Brightening

From where do we learn [the obligation to kindle] the Sab-
bath lamp? From [Isaiah 58:13] "And you shall call the Sabbath
joyful."
— Midrash Tanchumah, 58:1

Forget your perfect offering. There is a crack in everything.
That's how the light gets in.
— Leonard Cohen, "Anthem"
(adopted from a poem by Rumi)

I repose in myself. And that part of myself, that deepest and
richest part in which I repose, is what I call "God."
— Etty Hillesum (from her diary, *An Interrupted Life*)

WHEN I WAS GROWING UP, candle lighting seemed the consolation
prize for us girls who could not don tefillin. At least that's how I perceived it. When the Lubavitcher Hassidim (known for their Jewish out-
reach) came into town to show boys and young men how to wrap tefillin,
they handed out sets of candlesticks to the girls. To this day, I can picture them right in front of me: a pair of gold-colored metal candlesticks,
each with a gold ring dividing the base from the holder. Was the ring
symbolic of our future roles as wife, mother, and homemaker?

I felt slighted when I was given my set of candlesticks. The boys' tefillin looked interesting and special; the candlesticks looked flimsy. And
besides, three times daily I recited the Shema with its command to bind
tefillin on one's arms and head, but the only time I heard about Shabbat
candles in the prayer service was on Friday nights when we mumbled
Bameh Madlikin, the chapter from the Mishnah enumerating which oils
are permitted for lighting the Sabbath lamp. There is no question that
the Shema is considered a more important prayer than *Bameh Madlikin*.

Moreover, *Bameh Madlikin* presents candle lighting in the form of a
threat: If women are not scrupulous in the performance of this mitzvah,
according to this chapter of Mishnah, they will die in childbirth. No
surprise then that my associations with this mitzvah were not entirely
positive. Plus, the fact that the mitzvah of tefillin was off-limits to me
was a draw. If there is no woman in the house to do so, a man is still
required to light candles, while donning tefillin is a requirement of the
individual, not the household. As a young woman growing up in the
Orthodox world, I perceived this mitzvah to have nothing to do with me,
even forbidden. This made it all the more attractive.

And then there is the way these mitzvot were presented to me by my
parents. My mother took candle lighting as seriously as my father took
his mitzvah of tefillin. But when my brother became a bar mitzvah, it
was clear that he was to emulate my father and lay tefillin each morn-

ing. My parents bought him his own shiny new pair of tefillin. When I became bat mitzvah, no one bought me my own shiny new pair of candlesticks. Perhaps if they had, my relationship with this mitzvah might have been different. But this was not the way of my parents' community. Shabbat candle lighting was understood to be a ritual performed by the woman of the house in order to preserve "*shalom bayit*," peace in the home. In our community, it was assumed that we girls would not light Shabbat candles with our mothers when we reached the age of bat mitzah. Rather, we would start performing this mitzvah only when we had a house of our own.

Rabbi Yosi son of Rabbi Yehudah said: Two ministering angels accompany a person home on Friday night from the synagogue. One is an angel of good and one is an angel of evil. When the person arrives home to find the Shabbat candles lit, the table set and the beds made, the angel of good says, "May it be Your will that the next Shabbat should be the same." And against his will the angel of evil answers, "Amen."

If not [that is, if the candles are not lit and the table is not set], then the angel of evil says, "May it be Your will that the next Shabbat should be the same." And against his will the angel of good answers, "Amen."

— BT Shabbat 119b

The first Shabbat Jacob and I were home after our wedding, we lived in a middle-income housing project on the "Upper Upper" West Side of Manhattan. I was starting my senior year of college, and Jacob had just completed his studies. Our apartment had been Jacob's home before we married, and I moved in with him after the wedding. We were subletting from the owner.

We had invited guests over for dinner and planned to meet them at the synagogue. We lit Shabbat candles and went. When we returned, a strong smell of burnt debris filled the hallway and became stronger and stronger as we approached our apartment. When we reached the door, an angry woman was there waiting for us. We later discovered that she was the head of the housing project.

"Who are you?" she asked us. We told her that we lived in the apartment. She said that we were there illegally, that it was against the rules of the building to sublet the apartments. More importantly, we had caused a fire. We had left candles burning and apparently they had fallen over and set fire to something close by, perhaps the tablecloth. The fire department had come and put it out. Right in front of our Shabbat guests, this woman who felt like the angel of evil herself told us we now had three days to vacate the apartment. We had lit the candles and still the angel of evil had won out in our case, since the next Shabbat and many more Friday nights after that we did not dare to light Shabbat candles.

We were afraid to light the candles and go out, but we were also not willing to forgo Shabbat evening services to watch our candles burn. It felt to us that in our case lighting the candles would have compromised *shalom bayit* instead of improving it. A solution would have been for one of us to go and one of us stay home, which is what happened in my house when I was growing up. But that was not our vision for our Jewish life together. We wanted to go to shul together on Friday nights.

Suddenly, the impracticality of lighting Shabbat candles in a home with no distinct gender roles dawned on me. When I was growing up, it did not occur to me that lighting Shabbat candles could be dangerous. My mother never went to shul on Friday nights, so there was no problem. But our fire made me realize how the mitzvah assumes that the woman is staying home. In fact, as I began to tell our story, I heard others like it, some ending tragically. One family I met lost their entire house. Another lost a child.

Years later, while I was in shul for Kol Nidrei on Yom Kippur night, friends of ours were called out of shul by the police. Their candles had caused a fire in their home, destroying almost the entire interior and their belongings. And while it was a huge relief that they were all safe in shul during the fire, the mother, who does not frequent shul during the year because she suffers from an illness, began to ask herself if she could have prevented the fire if she had stayed home as usual. She felt guilty for going to shul with her family on Kol Nidrei night!

The danger of Shabbat candle lighting in a progressive religious community that values both men and women being in synagogue on Friday night is a serious matter whose resolution might shed light on the issue of gender roles in Judaism in general. Moreover, our fire made me wonder whether the wisdom and purpose of this ritual still stands. Originally, people took on the risk of fire when illuminating their houses in general. Now, we have a safer alternative for illumination. While it may be a beautiful idea to light candles before Shabbat and have them burning on the Sabbath table, risking a fire is certainly not conducive to *shalom bayit*. Neither is being put in a position where the couple must decide who will go to Shabbat evening services and who will stay home from synagogue to make sure a fire does not ensue. In a period when gender roles were distinct, this would not have been an issue, whereas now it is. As times change, the meaning projected by our rituals can change as well, or alternatively, the original meaning behind a ritual can become obsolete. Or sometimes the changing circumstances surrounding a ritual can create a situation where the ritual may have a different, or even opposite, effect than it was meant to have. In some cases the solution to this problem is to preserve the ritual but imbue it with new meanings; in other cases the solution is to change the ritual or the nuances in the way we practice it.

When asked if it is necessary in our modern age of electricity to light Sabbath candles, Rabbi Moshe Feinstein answered that it is necessary, since there may be a blackout and since it would feel like something is missing without Shabbat candles. Yet, if someone has only enough money to buy wine or candles for Shabbat, one should buy the wine and recite the blessing on the electric lights in the house. In addition, it has become customary for people staying in a hotel for Shabbat to light candles in the main dining hall but to keep in mind the electric lights in the hotel room when reciting the blessing. It seemed to me and Jacob, then, that when there is a fear of fire one should be able to recite the blessing on the electric house lights. This solution may perhaps not satisfy traditionalists, but it did provide a safe alternative and a modern answer to our complex problem.

On six days you shall work, but on the seventh day you shall
have a Sabbath of complete rest, holy to the Lord… You shall
kindle no fire throughout your settlements on the Sabbath day.
— Exodus 35: 1-3

Nowhere in the Torah are we told to light candles for Shabbat. We are told only that we are forbidden to kindle a fire on Shabbat itself.[1] How did lighting Shabbat candles become a mitzvah? And how did a ritual so totally time-bound become specifically a women's mitzvah?

An early midrash[2] suggests that it was not always obvious that one was even allowed to light a lamp before Shabbat to burn Friday night. The text asks if one should be forbidden to light a lamp or wrap food to keep it warm on Friday before sunset in order to benefit on Shabbat. The answer given is that one is permitted, because the prohibition regarding fire relates only to the act of lighting, not to benefiting from a lamp kindled before Shabbat.

Two more early Talmudic sources suggest that lighting a lamp before Shabbat was the common practice. Mishnah Shabbat 2:7 states that a person should make sure three things get done as the sun sets on Friday evening, one of which is the lighting of a lamp. This source can be read in two ways. Lighting the lamp can be seen as a utilitarian act meant to light up the home on Shabbat to make the holiday more enjoyable. We are told that Rav Hunah would light candles to prepare for Shabbat, which could be understood not as the Sabbath lamp itself, but as a preparatory measure for Shabbat so that the house would not be dark on Friday night. Alternatively, lighting the Sabbath lamp can be seen as a preventative act, one that we are told to complete before Shabbat so that we won't be tempted to light a lamp on Shabbat itself.

This latter reading would also be the most appropriate interpretation of the previous Mishnah (Shabbat 2:6, part of the *Bameh Madlikin* prayer), which tells us that women die in childbirth as a punishment for not be-

---

[1] Exodus 35: 3
[2] *Mekhilta DeRabbi Yishmael*, Vayakhel, Parashah 1

ing meticulous regarding three mitzvot: separating challah, observing the laws of *nidah*, and lighting the Sabbath lamp. This mishnah stresses the importance of being careful, or scrupulous, which suggests a concern that if the woman were to perform these mitzvot incorrectly she might bring grave punishment upon herself and her husband.

I choose this reading of the mishnah because the other two mitzvot—challah and *nidah*—are also in the woman's domain, but, as with this mitzvah, if she fails to perform them properly, her husband will be led to transgression: In the case of challah, he will sin by eating the portion of the dough meant for the Priests (challah); and in the case of *nidah*, he will sin by having sexual intercourse with a woman in *nidah*. Similarly, if the woman does not kindle the lamp before Shabbat, she or her husband may come to light it on Shabbat itself, transgressing the serious biblical prohibition against lighting a fire on the Sabbath. Or if she lights the lamp even a few minutes after Shabbat starts, he will be sinning when he benefits from that light.

By the later Talmudic period, lighting the Sabbath lamp adopted new meanings. The Gemara tells us that Shabbat candle lighting is meant to foster peace in the home–*shalom bayit*–on Friday night. Later commentators explain: If the house were dark, people would trip and quarrel.

The Gemara also introduces the ideas *kevod Shabbat* (honoring the Sabbath) and *oneg Shabbat* (enjoying the Sabbath) with regard to candle lighting. Candle light creates a festive atmosphere—think of a fancy candle-lit dinner.

Of course, before electricity all dinners were candle-lit. It would be disrespectful for the Sabbath to be the one night without light during the meal. Compare camping with a fire to camping without a fire. Trying to eat an outdoor meal at night without light (or warmth in cool weather) may not be impossible, but it is not pleasant and it certainly is not appropriate for a special occasion. But eating a meal around a camp fire is festive, cozy, and inviting. In keeping with this notion, Midrash Tanchumah says explicitly that the mitzvah of Shabbat candle lighting comes from Isaiah 58:13: "And you shall call the Sabbath joyful."

In medieval times, there was disagreement as to whether Shabbat candle lighting is a real mitzvah with a proper blessing. Rabbeinu Tam—a

12th century French scholar and grandson of the great sage known as Rashi—ruled that candle lighting is a mitzvah that must be performed right before Shabbat with the proper blessing. His became the accepted position; thus, the mitzvah became the ritual that ushers in Shabbat. Of course, it is practical to push off lighting the Sabbath candles until the last moment so the candles would last longer into Shabbat night.

Rabbeinu Tam writes about his sister (whose name was Chanah). She relays the custom of the women in her family of first lighting the candles and then, with the candles burning, reciting the blessing. This is remarkable for manifesting the reverse order of how most mitzvot with blessings are traditionally performed. Usually, one starts with the blessing and then performs the act. Chanah's blessing is the same one we recite today: *Baruch Atah Adonai, Eloheinu Melech Haolam, asher kidishanu bimitzvotav, vitzivanu, lihadlik ner shel Shabbat*, Praised are You, Lord our God, Sovereign of the Universe, Who sanctified us with Your mitzvot, and commanded us to kindle the Sabbath lamp. The halakhic authorities of the time relied on Chanah's testimony that this was the custom in her grandfather Rashi's household. They declared this custom halakhah.

Thus utilitarian candle lighting became the final act signifying the transition from *chol* (the routine) to *kodesh* (the sacred), the way that the Havdalah ritual (another ritual involving light) signifies the transition from *kodesh* to *chol* after Shabbat is over. There is tension among more recent halakhic authorities as to whether or not this ritual aspect of Shabbat candle lighting is a halakhically significant part of the mitzvah. Some say that it is and require that the candles be lit immediately before Shabbat, while others disagree and allow one to light the candles much earlier. According to these latter authorities, the timing of the lighting is insignificant, since what matters is that they provide light and a festive atmosphere and not that they serve the ritual function of transitioning from *chol* to *kodesh*.

In the modern age of electric lighting, the utilitarian aspect of the act of candle lighting is lost, since it is electric light and not candlelight that lights up the home. The ritual aspect comes to the fore. Shabbat candle lighting becomes the act that ushers in Shabbat. The *kevod Shabbat* and *oneg Shabbat* aspects are also stressed in halakhic responsa: The candles must be lit where one intends to eat one's dinner. This is not to provide light, but rather because the candles will add to the festive atmosphere of the Sabbath meal.

But why is this mitzvah considered more a "woman's mitzvah" than a man's? Especially considering that it is perhaps the most time-bound ritual act in all of Jewish praxis!

In each home, candles must be lit. It really makes no difference who lights them. In a home where there is only a man, he lights. But, it has become primarily the woman's responsibility to light the Shabbat candles in a home where there is both man and woman. Maimonides writes that it was only natural that the woman be the one to light the candles, because the home is the woman's sphere. (In fact, another name for woman in the Talmud is "*bayit*," house.)

In the Mishnah, we see that candle lighting is primarily the woman's responsibility. The Mishnah says that before Shabbat, a man should announce in his home (assuming that he has a wife, daughter, or mother living with him): "Light the candles!" (rather than do it himself). Later, by medieval times, the mitzvah is explicitly described by Maimonides as obligatory upon both men and women (both have the responsibility to make sure a lamp is lit in their household), but, he stresses, the woman is more commanded in this mitzvah than the man. In other words, it is both of their responsibility, but more so hers.[3]

Women in Eastern Europe composed Yiddish prayers to recite upon lighting the candles, and a halakhic penalty developed specifically for women who forgot to light before it was too late: they would be required to add one more candle each time they neglected to light on time.

Since my childhood ambivalence about Shabbat candle lighting, I have never managed to connect to this mitzvah in a deep way. Perhaps the fact that it is so incredibly time-bound puts into question for me the entire category of positive time-bound mitzvot. If I can not only be required to light Shabbat candles but required to do so more than my male counterparts, why can't I be required to don tefillin or recite the Shema prayer?

If I took the penalty of adding a candle after each missed lighting seriously, my candle tray would look like a shrine!

---

[3] *Mishneh Torah*, Hilkhot Shabbat 5:1-3

It is Friday afternoon in Jerusalem, and I have gone to the pool to swim laps before Shabbat.

A friend of mine is there too. "Are you also watching the clock?" she asks me. "I heard 5:08 is the outermost limit for candle lighting."

I explain that because I am meeting Jacob and the kids in shul and no one will be home to make sure the candles don't cause a fire, Jacob will say the blessing with the kids over the electric lights in the dining area as he sets up the lights in the house for Shabbat. "In our house, whoever is home recites the blessing. I don't rush home to be the one to do it," I add.

"Sometimes my husband lights for us too," my friend agrees. "But I do like to light my own, so if I can manage to get home in time, it's worth the rush. I think that is why I also wouldn't be satisfied with blessing over electric lights—although you're right; it is scary to think of what could happen. But I love the idea that I am doing this ritual like my Bubbe did, and my Alta-Bubbe before her. I would miss the magical moment of circling my hands over the flames and reflecting on the past week and throwing in some requests for the week to come."

My friend wishes me a "*Shabbat Shalom*," a peaceful Sabbath, and rushes out, leaving me wondering about my own relationship to this ritual.

I love the image of our family gathering around the burning candles and welcoming the Sabbath angels together; I wonder why it was so easy for me to let go of this ritual after the fire. Perhaps if I had tried harder, I would have been able to come up with a more creative solution than our current one of saying the blessing on the electric lights. Our idea makes sense; after all, it is the electric lights in the dining area that light up our Shabbat meal and give us *shalom bayit*. But we are missing that magical feeling of transitioning into Shabbat accompanied by the soft, natural candle light. That, and more. But what?

I envy my friend's connection to this mitzvah. Perhaps my alienation from Shabbat candle lighting lies deeper than my issues with the ritual itself. Perhaps I have resistance against the ritual that transitions us into

Shabbat because I am ambivalent about Shabbat. I must painfully admit that I am not always eager to welcome the Sabbath angels.

> *Rabbi Shimon ben Lakish says: The Holy One gives us an additional soul on Shabbat eve, and at the Sabbath's departure, it is taken from us, as is said, "The Sabbath ceased: va-yinafash."[4] Once the Sabbath ceases,* vay, ein nefesh: *"woe, the [additional] soul is no more."*
> — BT Taanit 27b

The Talmud tells us that on Shabbat we should wear special clothing set aside for only that day. Our conversation should be different on Shabbat. And we should eat special foods that we eat on that day alone. Shabbat should be a day totally different from any other day of the week. Even our thoughts should be different; they are meant to be directed towards lofty ideas and the immediate concerns of the Sabbath day.

In fact, a rabbi friend's father (also a rabbi) told her and her sisters when they were growing up that they could eat as much as they wanted on Shabbat, because Shabbat food has no calories!

Is this true? Do the calories from our food disappear on Shabbat? Is it possible to create a day totally different from any other? Can we push all of our very real concerns out of our minds for one day each week? And do we even want to? Do *I* want to?

> *If you want to use your relationship with food as the unexpected path, you will discover that God has been there all along. In the sorrow of every ending, in the rapture of every beginning. In the noise and in the stillness, in the upheavals and in the rafts of peace. In each moment of kindness you lavish upon your breaking heart... with each breath you take—God has been*

---

[4] Exodus 31:17

here. She is you.
— Geneen Roth, *Women, Food, and God*

After my last miscarriage, I felt deeply that I had put myself into God's hands, and this was liberating. I did not understand then that it was just a beginning. After I handed in my doctoral dissertation, I began planning the rest of my year. I finally had the time to write and to devote time to my rabbinical studies. Over the previous ten years or more, I had studied the laws of kashrut and *nidah*, and I had begun studying Shabbat—the final piece I needed to complete my studies for *smicha*, ordination. The time had come to complete Shabbat, get *smicha*, and move on in my life.

I established a plan to finish studying the laws of Shabbat privately, and to consult with my teachers when I had questions. But I also wanted to supplement my study of the halakhot of Shabbat with some study of the meaning of Shabbat. This felt essential to me. In addition to studying the actual laws, I felt I needed to look deeper. What was my relationship with halakhah? With ritual? With God? What kind of rabbi would I be? What did it mean for me to be a rabbi?

When I had begun my rabbinic studies over ten years earlier, I thought I knew the answers to those questions. But I had changed, the world had changed, and I was no longer certain of the answers. After years of thinking I could repair my small part of the world by fighting for equal access for women, especially in the world of halakhic Judaism where I felt most at home, I was beginning to question whether this would be enough. Lately, I had been feeling that the problems went much deeper than sexism. In fact, I had come to understand that sexism was merely a manifestation of these more essential problems and that equal access was merely a first step towards repair.

I was having basic doubts about the halakhic system and losing faith in the ability of the current rabbinic authorities to interpret and apply Torah in our modern world. The failure of the Orthodox world to change the nature of Jewish marriage from unilateral to bilateral to better reflect our modern understanding of marriage is one example of the failure. Another is couples who can't conceive because the woman ovulates before she can go the mikveh according to rabbinic law. Yet I experienced doubt not only in these extreme cases that pitted my moral sensibilities against my commitment to halakhah, but also in cases where my understanding of the spirit of certain mitzvot clashed with the rabbinic interpretation of how to practice those mitzvot. For reasons I had yet to discover, it was on Shabbat that I felt most potently the dissonance between spiritual ideal and practical application.

I knew that if I could find a way for my spiritual notion of Shabbat and my practice of Shabbat to meet, I would be closer to reaching the answers to those crucial questions about my relationship with halakhah, ritual and God. I decided, therefore, to study a more philosophical, spiritually-minded book about Shabbat to enhance my studies of the halakhot of Shabbat. By then, my CHaNaH group had disbanded. We had never gotten to the third mitzvah: *hadlakat ha-ner*, the lighting of the Sabbath lamp, but I asked one of the participants, Ruth (by then a rabbi), if she wanted to study with me.

We chose as our text Likutei Halakhot, a book written by Rabbi Natan, the student of Rabbi Nachman of Breslov, about the teachings of his rabbi. These writings fit into the category of Hassidut—spiritual, kabbalistic, devotional writings. The work is arranged by topic. I suggested that we begin with Shabbat. The opening section on Shabbat in Likutei Halakhot discusses eating. The Talmud[5] teaches that one must eat three meals on Shabbat. This is based on the appearance of the word "*yom*," day, three times in the verse telling the Israelites to collect the manna in the desert before Shabbat. In fact, the Talmud makes a big deal of these three meals. Rabbi Yossi, we are told, hopes to have his fate among those who eat the three meals of Shabbat with relish. And Rav Nachman says he is deserving of heavenly reward because he took special care to observe the practice of eating three special meals on Shabbat.

That leaves me cold. I eat only one meal on Shabbat.

In high school, I was diagnosed with a relatively rare neuromuscular disorder called FSHD: Fascio Scapular Humeral Muscular Dystrophy. The disease progresses slowly—from specific facial muscles to arm muscles to muscles in the torso and then to the legs—in most cases. It can

---

[5] BT Shabbat 117b

even progress to the lungs and other vital organs. It is a genetic disease, meaning that there is a 50% chance that each of my children has it. In fact, two of my children are already showing signs of the disease. I began to show signs when I was a child. I could not pucker my lips, blow up a balloon, or smile fully. But neither I nor my parents made much of it.

But then, in my third year of high school, I was suddenly unable to lift my arms above shoulder height. This was cause for concern. And so began months and months of doctor's appointments. We saw muscle doctors and bone doctors and neurologists. No one could explain what was going on. Finally, my cousin, a pediatric neurologist, sent us to a specialist. When I walked into this doctor's office, he took one look at me and said: "You have FSHD." I felt relief and anxiety. Finally, I knew what was wrong. It had a name. But at the same time, I suddenly became a person with a disease.

The doctor explained to us the developmental course of the disorder, and said that it would be impossible to predict how severe my case would be. Only time would tell. And, he added, there is no treatment for the disease. The only recommendations he could offer were staying thin and swimming. Excess weight puts unnecessary pressure on those muscles weakened by the disease. And, he added, his patients who swim regularly seem to do better, probably because they are keeping the muscles unaffected by the disease in good shape without putting too much strain on the affected muscles.

Since I was diagnosed with this disease, I have developed a peculiar eating habit as a way of retaining control over my weight. I eat only one meal a day: dinner. During the day, I drink: juices, milk, tea, coffee, and water. But I do not eat, even socially, until nightfall. I know there are other ways to control my weight, but this is what works for me. And it does not present a problem during the week; but on Shabbat it can be uncomfortable. When we are invited to friends' homes for lunch, I sit at the table, but I do not eat. This raises questions, and I answer them. Sometimes I think that it would be much simpler if I just ate lunch on Shabbat, but this is a habit I am not willing to let go of, despite the fact that it comes into conflict with traditional Sabbath observance.

When I researched the tradition of eating three meals on Shabbat, I learned that the reason behind this tradition is that Shabbat is supposed to be a special day, a day of celebration. And how do we show that we are celebrating? By eating well and eating more. But my relationship with food is too complicated for eating more than usual to be pleasurable.

Rabbi Nachman was an advocate of fasting during the week, because eating, he felt, feeds the *yetzer harah*, or the *sitra achrah*, the evil part of us. He felt strongly that there is a holy way of eating and a non-holy way of eating. Eating on Shabbat is a holy way of eating; it does not feed the *yetzer harah*. Rather, it feeds only the good part of us. It does the work that fasting does on Yom Kippur and that the shofar does on Rosh Hashanah. It wakes us up from our slumber and feeds our spirituality.

This made me wonder: If on Shabbat we don't feed the *yetzer harah*, then people with overeating disorders can feel free on Shabbat to eat foods they can't usually allow themselves to eat. They are not feeding their addictions because Shabbat is a day off from addiction. Similarly, perhaps I could allow myself to eat on Shabbat without worrying about losing control over my eating, gaining weight, and consequently quickening the pace of my muscular deterioration. Eating might have a totally different quality on Shabbat than it does during the week.

Perhaps I could bring myself to a higher spiritual realm if I were able to free myself of the need to control my food intake, at least on Shabbat, I told myself. Studying Rabbi Nachman's approach to eating on Shabbat made me wonder: *Would letting go of my need to control my eating on Shabbat be a step towards feeling freed around food? Could this be a road to healing? I say I have given myself over to God, but have I really? I say I trust in God, but do I with all of my soul if I still hold on to this controlling behavior?*

After my last miscarriage and the ritual I created around it, I felt I had handed myself over to God, come to trust in God, and admit my powerlessness in this world of unknowns. Yet I was still holding on to some of my controlling behaviors. I shared these thoughts with my hevruta. Experienced in spiritual counseling and healing, she told me I had inadvertently re-enacted the first three of the 12 steps at the heart of Alcoholics Anonymous and other recovery groups. My miscarriage experience had brought me to these first three steps on my own.

This raised the question: Should I continue to step four?

"Make a fearless and searching inventory of yourself."

I decided the time was ripe. I was open to looking deeper into what made it so difficult for me to allow myself to eat before dinner time even on Shabbat. And in order to do so, I knew I had to confront another of my addictive behaviors—this one perhaps even more extreme than the other: my attachment to my daily swim.

My eating habits were not the only thing that changed after I was diagnosed with FSHD. I also became a swimmer.

I swim every day for at least an hour. I used to swim every day except Shabbat. But when I was pregnant with my fifth child, Nachum, I felt I needed to swim on Shabbat as well. Because I was not swimming, my body felt weaker on Shabbat. I had less energy. And my general mood was less positive. Instead of being my most enjoyable day of the week, Shabbat became a day I resented. So I decided that I would start swimming on Shabbat as well.

But swimming is an activity that is traditionally considered not in the spirit of Shabbat in my religious community. There is no direct prohibition against swimming on Shabbat, but the Rabbis do, nevertheless, have a substantial list of concerns related to swimming—all of which are not especially applicable to the kind of recreational swimming people do today. The rabbinic objections reflect how in the Talmud's time, swimming, bathing, and boating were interconnected activities. Yet, most even liberal Orthodox Jewish communities do not make swimming part of their normal Sabbath activity.

This negative attitude towards swimming on Shabbat stems from one approach to Shabbat that is especially prevalent in the Orthodox world, which is that Shabbat should be a more dignified, more formal day than weekdays are. For example, one should dress in the kind of clothing one would wear to a fancy party and stay in that clothing all day long. For them, this is an expression of *"kevod Shabbat,"* the honor of the Sabbath. With that model in mind, it is easier to understand a resistance to activities like swimming and playing sports on Shabbat.

Yet I do not accept this approach to Shabbat. For me, relaxing means being comfortable and letting loose in some ways. So while I do dress in special clothing that I wear only on Shabbat when going to synagogue, I change into more comfortable clothing after services. Otherwise, Shabbat would feel oppressive to me, not enjoyable. So, for me, activities like swimming, playing sports, and hiking are among the most "*Shabbosdik*" (appropriate for Shabbat) activities there are. In fact, anything recreational to me feels appropriate for Shabbat—a day that I feel is about getting out of my regular "productive" routine and making time for other kinds of less "productive" but no less important activities.

This is how I feel about swimming on Shabbat. Yet all of my regular swimming friends who consider themselves religious do not even have a Shabbat membership at the pool—even those friends who swim every other day of the week. So when I walk to the swimming pool on Shabbat afternoons (it is not open on Saturday evenings; if it were, that would solve my problem), I hope no one will ask me where I am going. I would not lie. I am not ashamed to admit that I swim laps on Shabbat. But I do find it uncomfortable when people ask and look surprised when I tell them where I am headed.

It seems I am not totally at peace with my decision to start swimming laps on Shabbat, even though I know that I have a good medical reason for my decision. Deep down inside, I know that I cannot control the progression of my disease. But there is no doubt that swimming is good for me. When I swim, I can move in ways I can't outside of the water, stretch my muscles and exercise my limbs without putting too much pressure on my weak body. This is why my doctor recommended swimming as the best "medicine" for my disease. And swimming helps me psychologically deal with the fact that I have an incurable disease that may end up handicapping me in more serious ways than it already does. Swimming makes me feel that I can at least do something to take care of myself. It relaxes me, clears my mind, and opens me up into acceptance of what is. For me, swimming is meditation.

Yet, perhaps it is because swimming is so important to me that I have mixed feelings about my decision to make lap swimming part of my Shabbat. There is a rabbinic prohibition against healing on Shabbat. This is curious, considering that the halakhah allows for medical reasons to break the laws of the Sabbath. This is because once one has a medical excuse one is outside the realm of Shabbat and therefore can break the laws of Shabbat (and another person can break these laws to heal you)— not that healing itself is in the spirit of Shabbat.

On the surface, the prohibition against healing on Shabbat is a result of the fact that there are people whose profession it is to heal others; therefore, healing is considered "work". On a deeper level, healing is a form of fixing, which is also not considered in the spirit of Shabbat. I wonder if on a more spiritual level, my decision to start swimming laps on Shabbat is not in tune with what I really feel Shabbat is all about, because it's not an act of "letting go," of breaking free of routine and dependencies, but rather of relying on what is most comfortable, of asserting control in a world that is really so far from being in my control. Moreover, it means letting my everyday worries enter into my Shabbat.

Since Shabbat is supposed to be both our most pleasurable day, and a day different from all other days, of the week, I am in a bind. If I don't swim on Shabbat, I suffer. If I do swim on Shabbat, I am letting my everyday routine structure my Shabbat. Wouldn't it be nice to have one day a week when swimming did not matter, when I could free myself of this need? Yet, it is a very real need of mine. My disease does not disappear on Shabbat. And while swimming will not cure my FSHD, it does seem to be helping me stay in good shape physically and mentally despite the disease. Why deprive myself of this on the one day of the week that is supposed to be the most pleasurable of all?

One wintery Saturday afternoon, the Shabbat before the holiday of Chanukkah, I went to hear my friend, Rute, a teacher of Hassidut, teach a class on the Ishbitzer Rebbe, who lived in the late 18th and early 19th centuries. The topic of this class was the Ishbitzer's notions of *bayit*, home.

She began by talking about how Chanukkah, the holiday of rededicating the Temple, is the holiday of *bayit*. The Talmud tells us that the mitzvah of Chanukkah candle lighting is an obligation for a person (the word is "*ish*", man, in the Talmud, but elsewhere in the Gemara it is concluded that women are also obligated in this mitzvah) and his/her home, "*bayit.*" This means that Chanukkah candle-lighting is a home-based mitzvah. One is meant to light the candles at home or wherever one considers oneself at home (or the halakhah considers one at home). In fact, if you are abroad, someone else who lives in the house can fulfill the requirement for you by keeping you in mind while lighting at home.

Rute presented us with her interpretation of the Ishbitzer's various models of being at home. Abraham, when he left his home and was told to go to "the Land that God would show him," was also told to sever himself from everything that was familiar to him—his habits, his surroundings, his routine, his friends, and family—so that he could grow into his true self. In fact, the Ishbitzer understands the double language of "going" to mean that Abraham is being commanded to go to himself. "*Lech lechah,*" commanded God, which can be translated as "Go to yourself." In other words, God commands him to leave in order to become himself.

Based on her study of the Ishbitzer's other teachings, Rute felt that the Ishbitzer's approach to Abraham's mission could not be quite so straightforward. Rute therefore offered her own reading of the Ishbitzer. Or, to be more accurate, her own elaboration of what the Ishbitzer wrote based on other passages of his elsewhere in his writings.

According to Rute's understanding, Abraham's journey away from home was not a total severing, because Abraham was going "from (*mi*)" all of this to himself. In order to become himself, he needed to stay connected to where he came from. He would build from his home base rather than totally break with his past.

Rute shared with us how this interpretation of Abraham's mission helped her when she was coming back to Israel after living in New York for a number of years while her husband was in medical school. Rute found it hard to believe that she was meant to leave all of her experiences behind when she left America. Her experiences in America helped her grow into the mature, multi-faceted person she is now. Her horizons were broadened, and she gave birth to her oldest children when she was

there. Rather, she was certain the Ishbitzer would have told her to bring
all of her experiences, all she had learned during her sojourn, along with
her in her suitcase.

The next teaching Rute brought was the Ishbitzer's commentary on
Deuteronomy 12:20, where Moses tells the Israelites that God will expand their borders. The Ishbitzer points out that God does not say that
the Israelites will go beyond their borders, but rather that their borders
will be expanded. Putting this in the context of home and feeling at
home, Rute explained that we can change and grow without crossing
our own borders, because, like a woman in her childbearing years, our
physical borders can expand and contract as per our changing needs.
Humans stretch their own personal boundaries according to the specific
circumstances of their lives. People can grow and change without losing
their essence.

To illustrate this point, Rute explained how this teaching was essential
when she left Israel for America. She was afraid to go, afraid she would
lose her religious Zionist identity, afraid she would not remain herself
outside of Israel. But the Ishbitzer's teaching helped her realize that she
could expand her own borders without losing herself in the process.

Finally, Rute brought one of the Ishbitzer's teachings on the death of
Nadav and Avihu, Aaron the Priest's two sons, who were struck down
by God when they offered a "strange," or unrequested, sacrifice. But why
did they have to die?

The verse in Numbers 3:4 tells us that Nadav and Avihu had no sons.
This, Rute explained, sheds light on why they could not return to earth.
They came close to God, but they had no anchor, no home, to return to.
They were not married. They had no children. The point of this teaching
is that in order to safely grow as a human being in this world, one must
understand one's borders; otherwise one may simply break through one's
borders instead of pushing them to expand in a healthy way. One needs
a home base from which to grow.

As I sat in this class, I felt the Ishbitzer speaking to me through Rute's
interpretations. As I took my personal inventory, I had been wondering
if my story could be a metaphor for the Jewish female experience. As a
girl stifled by her place in traditional Judaism and by halakhah in general,

I feared losing myself in this system. I knew that I needed to break free of the control the Modern Orthodox Jewish community of my childhood had over me. I felt that "society" (as represented by the community in which I was enmeshed as a child) was asking me to sacrifice my true self.

Then I went off to college and felt I had escaped my religious identity. I lived a life devoid of tradition, unfettered by halakhah and, for a short while, I felt free. Then I began to doubt that my newly found freedom allowed for my true self to emerge. If discovering one's life dreams and connecting to one's deepest core were as simple as rebelling against authority figures and breaking away from social norms, my troubles would have been over. But I began to feel disconnected. I experienced an emptiness that I thought could only be filled by reconnecting to my tradition. I thought if I could find a way to live in my tradition but also express myself as an individual, I would be cured.

I became a traditional religious woman who prayed with tallit and tefillin and studied to become an Orthodox rabbi. This role suited me, because it allowed me to remain within the traditional community in which I had been raised while still expressing my discontent with the status quo. I saw myself as an archetype for Jewish women in many ways. We could cure what was wrong with Judaism by taking on mitzvot traditionally performed only by men and taking our Judaism seriously— studying Torah, and writing ourselves back into the tradition.

I managed to find a way to live in the halakhah, in tradition, but I did not get to the root of the problem. While I knew that a total break with tradition was not the answer, I was beginning to think that trying to fit into the traditional system that men had created was not the answer either. I felt that my voice was still being stifled, or more accurately, that I was silencing my own voice in order to earn social acceptability.

Change has to go both ways. Of course we all have to make some adjustments in order to "fit in" and "get along"—that is what living in community is all about—but when the adjustments are all one-sided, when we are forced to sacrifice our true selves to an unhealthy degree, that is when psychoses arise. As I now saw it, the sacrificing was unbalanced in the halakhic Jewish world. And it was not just women who were suffering. Society as a whole suffers when not all of its members are given a voice and when those with less power are made to comply with unjust rules to preserve the status quo deemed for the "general good" by those in power.

My personal inventory helped me discover that searching for the lost voice inside of me and Judaism would mean looking in places I was not accustomed to going. It meant opening up to new religious and spiritual experiences. It meant allowing myself the freedom to step outside of the traditional halakhic framework. Rute's interpretation of the Ishbitzer's notion of home helped me realize that I need not fear embarking on this journey, because I could stretch my boundaries without breaking through them. I had to make room for the Divine Light that was within me to shine through. I could remain connected to the tradition but find my own individual expression within that framework to a larger extent than I had allowed myself to dare. Until now, I had fought within the system. In order to hear CHaNaH's voice, I would have to summon the courage to break some rules.

I had to let go of my need for approval, because there was a good chance that I would lose that approval if I truly listened to what CHaNaH's voice had to say. My parents would not approve of my choices, and the liberal halakhic community of which I still considered myself a member would say I had gone too far.

I heard Chanah speaking to me through Rute that Shabbat afternoon. Breaking rules does not necessarily mean breaking boundaries. When done with care, sensitivity, and holy intention, breaking rules can be an activity of expansion, of building, of growth, rather than of destruction.

> R. Hiyya the Elder and R. Simeon ben Halafta were walking in the valley of Arbel and saw the light of daybreak. R. Hiyya the Elder said to R. Simeon: Eminent master, Israel's redemption will be like this—little by little at the beginning; but as it advances, it will grow larger and larger.
> — JT Berachot 1:1

Now that I had completed the first five Recovery steps (the fifth being sharing my new-found discoveries with myself, others, and God), it was time to move on to the sixth step: to be ready to let God remove my addictions. *Was I ready for this huge step?* I asked myself. Perhaps if I didn't think of it as such a huge step, perhaps if I took one tiny step at a time, I would be able to at the very least begin the process.

I thought of Rabbi Hiyya the Elder looking out at daybreak, as the light began to peak up through the horizon, and how he saw in this a model for the gradual bringing of the redemption. If I began to let the light shine through, I would eventually see the bright sun that would illuminate my existence. It was time for me to set in motion a series of small steps towards my own redemption.

Do I have the courage to expand my boundaries the smallest bit so that I can begin to let the light of daybreak shine through? I asked myself.

Before the mirror, my body looks alien to me: My arms and shoulders and legs are skinny, no muscles to speak of. My shoulder blades wing out. My stomach protrudes. *Whose misshapen, disproportioned, sickly body is this?* I wonder.

Walking is hard lately. I trip and fall often enough for concern. I can't seem to keep my balance. My two-year-old son tackles me with a love-hug, and I fall over. I have to tell him to be careful: "*Ima* is not so sturdy, Nachum. You have to be gentle."

I decide to go to the doctor, although I know there is nothing he can do. I feel that somehow by checking in with him, I am at least acknowledging the disease's progression. He says I am lucky to still be walking on my own two feet at age 36. He says I could still be walking in twenty years, or I could be in a wheelchair, or worse. What am I supposed to do with that kind of information?

I ask him if there is any reason for me not to consider having another child. He says: "I can't tell you that. It's for you to decide. Of course pregnancy, childbirth, and raising a child takes a toll. But how much, I can't say. I am a doctor, not a prophet. We know so little about this disease. You probably know better than I do. You live with it."

I read the FSHD Society newsletter. Among articles about raising money, lobbying Congress, and medical research, there are two obituaries: A 13-year-old boy and a 42-year-old woman. Both died of the disease. The woman had respiratory trouble. They do not explain why exactly the boy died. But I won't necessarily die of this disease. There is no way to predict the progression of FSHD. Not knowing is, perhaps, the hardest part. But maybe that is also what helps me push on. I am partially in denial. But feeling how my condition worsened makes it harder and harder to continue in that mode. Moreover, I worry about those two of my children who also have the disease.

As my FSHD has progressed, leaving me less and less mobile, more and more weak, part of me wants to move to the Rockies or the Alps and spend time in nature every day and write—before it's too late. Forget about being a rabbi and living in Jerusalem and maybe even forget about halakhic Judaism. Do I have the strength to go on? At what point should I say "enough!" and stop and enjoy, because who knows for how much longer I'll be able to do those things even I tend to take for granted?

Rabbi Nachman of Breslov, himself a sickly man who died young, plays on the Hebrew term for a long life, "*arichut yamim*," literally a length of days. He tells us that living a long life is not measured in years alone, but in making each day long. He says that the day begins short, with few hours and much to accomplish. But, if we infuse each hour, each moment, with holiness, we can make the day longer. And in such a way, we make our lives longer; if not in a literal, physical way, then in a spiritual, metaphysical way. But how can I infuse each and every moment of my life with holiness? I wonder. That is the challenge.

How can my life outlook not change as my disease progresses? My vulnerability and the fleeting nature of life become more apparent each day. The big picture feels more important, the little details less so. That, I think, is why I have more trouble with the intricacies of halakhah. My relationship with God occupies my religious energy more and more now. But I have to believe that these two can go hand in hand—a life guided by halakhah and a life of the spirit. I feel compelled at this point in my life to find balance and harmonize these two aspects of being Jewish, because both are important.

Rabbi Joseph Soloveichik, the preeminent rabbinic figure of the 20th century, writes about Religious Man vs. Scientific Man vs. Halakhic Man. Religious Man has no grounding and Scientific Man has no spirit. Halakhic Man has both. The significance of a mitzvah, he says, is not in the feeling it evokes, but in the actual performance in its detailed exactitude. While a surge of religious feeling may be subdued by this cold exacting attitude, one is compensated by the joyous sense of dedication that accompanies the performance of these tasks.

Rabbi Soloveichik considers it inevitable that sometimes halakhah does not jibe with spiritual expression, that sometimes the two are in sync and sometimes they are not. But sometimes is not enough for me. I want that surge of religious feeling. I want my spiritual life to coincide with my religious life at all times. I want them to be totally in sync. I also want my ethical and ideological life to be in sync with my religious life. I want my actions to always be guided by my spiritual, ethical, and religious conscience. And I want Judaism to be a progressive, redemptive force in the world, not a regressive, oppressive one.

I know I feel committed to living in a relationship with the unfolding mythical story of my people and our history. I also know I feel God guiding me almost daily. But I am not sure how much my relationship with God and my religious practice are connected. I strive to make them connect more, and I see doing so as part of my Jewish feminist journey. I see this as the main goal of religious feminism, because including Chanah in the religious project should bring the balance we have been lacking until now. Without this balance, we have been a people deaf in one ear. We could not clearly hear God's voice being channeled through humanity when half of humanity was left out. As a woman and a rabbi in the 21st century, I consider it my mission and responsibility to begin to make Chanah's voice heard so that God's Voice can someday be heard as well.

The question is: How?

We are told in the Gemara[6] that Rabbi Elazar said in the name of Rabbi Yossi ben Zimra that if a person fasts on Shabbat, the heavenly court will annul any harsh rulings upon that person from the rabbinic court. Ritvah, Rabbi Yom Tov ben Avraham in 13th century Spain, explains that this is because fasting on Shabbat, when others are enjoying themselves, is especially difficult and therefore has special power and influence in the heavenly realm.

Immediately preceding this radical statement on a Shabbat fast, the same scholars present a midrash: The Rabbis recall a phrase from the story of Chanah's praying for a son. "And Chanah, she spoke on her heart." The midrash plays off the phrase "*on* her heart": Chanah said before God: "Creator of the World! All that you created in woman, none of it was for naught. Eyes to see, ears to hear, a nose to smell, a mouth to speak, arms to work, legs to walk, breasts to suckle with. These breasts that you placed upon my heart: for what are they if not to suckle? Give me a son, and I will suckle him with them!"

On first read, it seems that the reason the Gemara juxtaposes the discussion of fasting on Shabbat with this midrash about Chanah's mode of prayer is that they are both quoted in the name of the same two rabbis. However, I wonder if there is not a deeper connection between fasting on Shabbat and Chanah praying "on her heart." Both are unconventional acts of spiritual expression that these rabbis cast in a positive light.

Chanah is our model for authentic prayer because she prayed from her heart rather than from a codified text. Could this serve as a model for meaningful ritual in general? When one is looking to experience an authentic Shabbat—or any ritual or religious observance for that matter—could it be that sometimes looking into one's heart, rather than simply into the books of religious law, is what is most called for?

In the "Women in Halakhah" course I teach, I usually have the same students from class to class, but sometimes I have a visitor—a person visiting Israel for a short time who wants to study some Torah, or a

---

[6] BT Berachot 31a

parent, grandparent, sibling, or friend of one of my students. Usually they enhance the class, which was certainly the case with one particular guest.

When I walked into class, there he was. A svelte man of about fifty with clear gray eyes, bearded yet clean-cut, dressed in a plain suit. He sat there, eager to learn. He wore a knitted *kippah* on his head, and his familiarity with the language and texts was obvious. As the class continued, it became more and more apparent that he had studied Jewish legal texts intensively in the past. He jumped right in—contributing, even correcting and critiquing, but all with a self-effacement and modesty that left it clear who was the teacher and who the student. I liked him. His smile and excitement were contagious. When the other students left, he remained. He wanted to talk. He was charged by the Torah study, I could see in his sparkling eyes. "How did you research this subject?" he wanted to know. "It's been so many years since I've done any serious studying. Did you write a book, some articles?" He was waiting with pen in hand to write down whatever he could.

I explained that I did write a book, and that I was also happy to send him all of my sources for the course by e-mail. He was so grateful, it was touching. "So where did you study?" I asked.

I recognized the name of the institution. It was the same Modern Orthodox rabbinical seminary I had applied to over ten years earlier as a statement that women too should be allowed to study for Orthodox rabbinic ordination. "I got *smicha* there," he added, revealing that he had received Orthodox ordination. "But I don't like to tell people that, because I really don't consider myself Orthodox any longer. I'm not proud of what Orthodoxy has become, to tell you the truth."

This was getting interesting. "How so?" I probed.

"Well, to start with—prayer. That's my pet peeve. I am a hospital chaplain, you see. And I do a lot of praying with the patients. But we rarely use a siddur," he said, referring to a Jewish prayer book. "I don't always use one myself. I like to pray from the heart. When I went backpacking in New Hampshire, I brought my tefillin with me, but no siddur. I know a lot of it by heart, and the rest I preferred to improvise. To really talk to God. That's true prayer."

"Wow," I said.

"As I see it," the man continued, "We've totally lost what prayer is supposed to be about. We've lost Chanah, the model of prayer. She spoke from her heart. Now that was true prayer. What we do is a sorry attempt at trying to emulate her. We've created so many words and rules that it's impossible to truly pray with all of that structure.

"Here's an example: I sat with an elderly woman before I came here. She knew she was dying. It was only a matter of how many weeks. She was depressed. They had her on anti-depressants. I said to her: Florence, how would you like to be remembered when you're gone? She perked up when I asked her that. No one before me had even mentioned that she would be gone. But she wanted to talk about it, and I was someone she could do that with, safely."

"So what did Florence say?" I asked eager to hear the rest of this story.

"She said she wanted to be remembered as a giving person."

"That's beautiful."

"Then I asked her what she would ask for if she were to pray. She said she would ask God to make things easier for her now. So I told her that I was moved to pray, and would it be all right if I prayed then and there. She said yes. So I began to pray, in my own words. I said: God, I have Florence here with me, and she's leaving this world. She's been a giving person all her life, and now she has something to ask of you. Could you help make things easier for her now? She's having a hard time. She needs your help."

"Did it help her?"

"It was very powerful. The prayer really helped Florence get through those last weeks. But the reason that I'm telling you this story is that it was not about looking for which psalms best fit her situation. Those aren't our words; they're King David's words. And I don't even like his words so much, to tell you the truth. They certainly wouldn't have spoken to Florence. Do you see what I mean?"

What this rabbi was suggesting raised many issues for me relating not only to prayer, but to the general relationship between spiritual expression and halakhah—which particularly interested me in the context of Shabbat. Aspects of the traditional Shabbat experience—like not working on the computer or talking on the telephone—did seem totally appropriate to me, because we are so tied to our telephones and computers that it is truly spiritually, psychologically, and physically liberating to be free of them one day each week. But sometimes the rules of Shabbat are so picayune that they become counterproductive. Instead of expending my spiritual energy on reflecting on my week and focusing on all of my blessings, I was expending it on the details of which way the halakhah permits me to cut my salad, warm my food, or wash my dishes.

I understood that ideally, on Shabbat I should not be making a salad or washing my dishes at all because the Sabbath is meant to be a day of rest. But because it is also meant to be a day of enjoyment, the Rabbis allowed for these activities so that the day would not become one of deprivation. This attention to how we do these activities is meant to remind us of that fact; often, however, it does more to drain my spiritual energy. It is my belief that people have limited energy to expend on spiritual pursuits, and when that energy is used up on details, even if they do have some apparent meaning, we lose sight of the larger transformative picture. How much more is this true when the details don't even have apparent meaning—as is often the case with religious ritual today.

Sometimes halakhah is in tune with and conducive to spirituality. And sometimes it is not. This is simply the nature of living within a halakhic system. But after speaking to this man, I realized that I was not willing to accept a halakhah that did not enhance my life spiritually—except when I did see some other non-spiritual benefit for keeping the traditional way, such as remaining part of a community or connecting to tradition. But when the spiritual costs outweigh the social or sociological benefits—when ritual acts begin to feel stale and meaningless—I realized that I was no longer willing to toe the line.

We've lost Chanah, I heard this rabbi, this pastoral chaplain, tell me. We've lost spiritual immediacy. It's been lost in words and rules. It's no wonder that we can't connect to God properly through that morass.

It seemed to me that in a Jewish world preoccupied with halakhah and communal norms, we were losing sight of God. The former matter, but are problematic when communal norms stifle personal spiritual expression and even take the interpretation of mitzvot in a direction that seems further and further away from any transformative religious and redemptive ethical vision for the world. We need a healthy balance. That is Chanah's message. Today we have become like Eli the Priest who thought Chanah was drunk when he saw her praying. She was moving her lips, but he heard no voice, so he thought there was something wrong with her. He missed the point. He mistook her spiritual fervor for drunkenness. We tend to think people who talk about God, spirituality, and tikkun olam are either on drugs or insane. Or we question their seriousness or respectability. But as I listened to this rabbi, I wondered if these standards were set by a system that valued the intellectual over the emotional, words over feelings, laws over intuition. Listening to this rabbi, I was beginning to think I was coming closer to understanding Chanah's secret and hearing her silenced voice.

This rabbi went on to say that in Israeli hospitals, there are no chaplains. The rabbis on staff at hospitals worry about the kashrut and make sure the hospital synagogue runs properly. But they don't counsel patients. They are not available to guide them spiritually. That is not their job. And they would look suspiciously at anyone who claimed to be a rabbi who wanted to do that type of work. "What does that have to do with religion?" they would ask.

Has this obsession with the intricacies of the formalistic law, and the need to have everyone conform, become a means to avoid spirituality? This rabbi forced me to ask myself. I saw this in the Jewish community of my childhood. No one ever talked about God, but we knew what was forbidden and what was permitted. And this was not necessarily a bad thing; rules can be a road map for life if they are necessarily connected to the goal of being better, more ethical, more God-centered, more thoughtful human beings. But in a vacuum, they become problematic because they become an ends instead of a means.

I thought of the verse in Deuteronomy 30:12 that God's Law "is not in the Heavens." This phrase is interpreted in the Talmud[7] to mean that Torah exists only in so far as human beings interpret it. *Does this mean that once Torah has been interpreted by the Rabbis, the process ends? Should human interpretation be devoid of any larger spiritual and ethical picture?* I asked

---

[7] BT Baba Metzia 59b

myself. Of course not. Rather, I told myself, it is the responsibility of individual human beings in all times and places to critique interpretations they feel depart too much from what seems to them the Will of God.

We can lose sight of the bigger picture when we get caught up in following the rules. There is a strain of Jewish tradition that warns not to delve into the deeper meaning of laws out of fear one might decide the meanings are no longer meaningful and therefore abandon these practices. This approach closes us off to the development of new meanings and the adaptation of rules. This approach can get us stuck. As the world develops around us, we won't allow the rules to change organically along with the world. And so, the rabbinic rules, which are actually only meant to be a frame, a shell, a temporary means towards reaching the essence, could become an *empty* frame or shell.

I pictured this as a flame without that blue center, the hottest part of the fire. If the center of the flame is blue, the fire is going to continue to burn for some time. But if it is not, the fire is on its way to going out. We don't want our ritual to become a flame without its blue center; if it does, it is on its way to meaninglessness. And once it has lost its meaning, it is only a matter of time before it burns out.

By letting the shell become the essence itself, we are not only perpetuating ritual that has no meaning, but we are actually making the rules into an idol. We are guilty of *avodah zarah*, idol worship. This is what I understood with the help of this rabbi that Chanah would be screaming out: *"Listen to your inner voices, the sparks of God inside each and every one of you. Don't let the technicalities of the rules become the end rather than the means! Trust your instincts! Trust your ability to talk to God!"*

I thanked this rabbi visitor for joining my class, and we exchanged e-mail addresses. I hoped to hear more from him in the future, but I was not sure I would. He lived far away, in a remote part of the United States. I doubted our paths would ever cross again. But this added to the serendipitous nature of this encounter. This man felt to me like Elijah the Prophet himself. He had come from across the world to guide me, to help me get closer to my own inner truth. His work in the lives of others would continue to go on. But even if I never saw him again, he had done his work in my life.

I decided to attend a Friday night prayer service at the home of my rabbi friend Ruth, an invitation I had declined numerous times, fearing it would be too untraditional for my taste. These experimental services, which she organized once a month, were led each time by a different person with no commitment to stick to the traditional format. One could not be sure what was in store. Openness and flexibility were required.

My previous attempts to worship in a non-traditional style had not been fulfilling. They left out so much of the traditional service that I felt compelled to pray again when we returned home. But that was before I began to experience the traditional service as monotonous and repetitive, as weighing me down rather than lifting me up. I had begun to rethink my relationship to prayer. I needed a new window back in, a new way to talk to God. So I decided to attend my friend's services for the first time.

The approach to prayer I discovered that Friday night was one which saw no need to recite the entire text in the prayer book. Rather, specific prayers were selected and deeply experienced through chanting and movement. For instance, we spent at least twenty minutes chanting the following line from the Kabbalat Shabbat service: *"Mizmor shir leyom hashabbat. Tov lehodot la'Adonay ulezammer leshimkha elyon.* A song for the Shabbat day. It is good to thank God and sing to the Heavenly Name."

I found that this approach lifted me to heights in prayer that I had not reached before. Without all of those many words getting in the way, I could focus and let go. I could see that it was working for the people around me as well. I was moved to tears watching them swaying and dancing and jumping—standing and sitting spontaneously, as they felt moved to by the prayers, rather than as they felt compelled to because of some instructions written in the prayer book, or because everyone else around them was doing so. People were crying, laughing, calling out to God.

Opening myself up to this new kind of prayer experience was an important step towards discovering my Sabbath soul. I found that too many words all at once inhibited prayer's ability to free the additional soul that

I am granted on Shabbat. Once I let my Sabbath soul free to flow with the experience, I no longer felt weighed down by the tradition and the rabbis before me. I felt lighter; I could soar.

But while part of me longs for that kind of lightness of being, the freedom to reach higher heights, another part of me prefers to feel grounded. *Is there a way to feel grounded while still soaring? To feel connected but not bound?* I felt that this Shabbat was a step in that direction. I gave myself the freedom to explore. I gave myself room to move, to breathe, and to look inside myself at my own Divine Light. But that does not preclude the option of praying in more traditional settings at other times as well.

I left that Shabbat prayer experience asking myself this essential question: *How will I set my Sabbath soul free?* I had discovered that skipping parts of the service allowed me to focus on what I was saying and experiencing. I decided that I would not let my nostalgia for traditional prayer stand in the way of my search for a more meaningful Sabbath service. If I could find the most uplifting and exciting Shabbat worship in non-traditional groups such as this one, I would not let that stop me anymore.

To be willing to let go of the traditional service, its comfort and familiarity, required of me a willingness to let go of what has always been done. It required the courage to break with certain aspects of tradition in order to keep Torah fresh and relevant.

I had thought that like Nadav and Avihu's unrequested form of worship, praying in this untraditional way was crossing my boundaries rather than expanding them. But now, I experienced the holiness in this mode of prayer, and it became impossible for me to dismiss its power and relevance in the world's current spiritual reality.

Of course, there was also a sociological issue involved. Praying regularly in a prayer setting like this would put me outside the realm of what even the liberal halakhic community had decided was acceptable. But that did not bother me anymore. I wanted, through my prayer experience, to get closer to God; that became my priority in my new-found approach to ritual.

I needed to be woken from my walking slumber. As Rabbi Nachman of Breslov describes: "There are those people who sleep away their days."

Going to traditional prayer services week-in-and-week-out was starting to feel like a walking slumber. I didn't think I would want to pray in such an untraditional service every Shabbat. But once in a while, it seemed like a refreshing change. A wake-up call.

R. Simeon ben Lakish said: The Torah given to Moses was written with black fire upon white fire, sealed with fire, and swathed with bands of fire. While writing it, Moses wiped off the reed on his hair—thus he received the radiance that was to emanate from his countenance.
— Yalkut Shimoni, Berachah 951

The Shabbat of Parashat Vayishlach—when we read the Torah portion about the biblical Jacob's struggle with the mysterious "man" and his reconciliation (and parting of ways) with his brother, Esau—I decided to hold a "Family Prayer Service" in my home. Letting go of the traditional prayer format opened up a way for me to create a prayer service in which adults and children of all ages could feel welcomed and fulfilled.

I had been involved in various prayer communities over the years. I had even been involved in founding and running some of these communities. But none of them completely fulfilled my vision for a service that would meet most of my needs. The service in Ruth's home was only once-a-month on Friday nights. Moreover, it was not geared towards children. So many a Shabbat morning I spent in the children's service, and the truth is that often I did not feel frustrated being there. On the contrary, there were aspects of the children's service that I found refreshing. For one, gender was not an issue and politics and power were removed from the prayer experience. I appreciated the purity and innocence that existed in that environment, the spontaneity and the ease that was missing from the adult service. This service also reminded me of the more experimental services I had attended recently—fewer words and more singing. And so, I decided to finally put my vision into action.

I called friends to invite them to the service. It would be a shortened version with more singing and less silent reading, so the kids could participate and concentrate, with a pot luck lunch to follow. Michal and her friends would read from the Torah, and a theatrical woman friend of mine would perform a short skit on the weekly Torah portion. Over lunch, the adults and older children would discuss that week's Torah portion, while the younger children would play and eat outside in the garden.

Issues came up for me about women's participation and minyan (prayer quorum). There would not be ten men present, and so, could we recite the portions of the prayer service that require the presence of ten men, a traditional minyan? And if I did decide to count women in the minyan, would I allow women to lead those portions of the service that require a quorum? I struggled with myself as I made these decisions. As I prepared to lead the discussion on the Torah portion, I found help in the story about Jacob's enigmatic struggle with the mysterious "*ish*" (man). All we are told about this struggle is that it lasts until morning, and that when the struggle is over, although Jacob defeats the man, he is wounded in the process. He walks away limping.

With what or with whom is Jacob struggling? Studying the familiar story this time, I understood Jacob to be struggling with his controlling self. After all, Jacob is a controlling individual. He lives his life in a careful, measured way. His name, in fact, indicates that aspect of his character. When he and his twin brother Esau were born, Jacob came out second, holding on to Esau's ankle, in Hebrew his "*ekev.*" That is the reason for his name, Yaakov.

Jacob is not one to be at the forefront, the cutting-edge. He lags behind. He does not live passionately or spontaneously, the way his brother Esau does. But, as Avivah Gottlieb Zorenberg writes in the section on this Torah portion in her book, *Genesis: the Beginning of Desire*: "To be obsessed with controlling the issues in a complex world is to risk losing all dynamic contact with that world."[8]

Jacob struggles to break free of this aspect of himself. He needs to learn to live in the moment, open himself up, make himself vulnerable to perhaps even being hurt; because only that is truly living. This is why Ja-

---

[8] JPS, 1995, p. 233.

cob emerges from the struggle, this internal struggle with himself, limping. He needs to learn to give up control. Maybe he will go through the rest of his life limping, but he is now internally whole. He may be hurt, but he is wholly himself. He is Israel, the name God bestows upon him when he emerges from this struggle.

As I read, I saw myself in Jacob. I felt the two sides of me—the Jacob side, which needs to control and be controlled, that needs order and careful thinking and planning—and the Israel side—which lives in the moment, acts with passion and spontaneity—wrestling it out. And I knew that like the biblical Jacob, I would have to go to that place deep inside myself and enter into that struggle.

I knew I may come out of this struggle vulnerable and even wounded. I may risk rejection. I may risk public scrutiny. I may risk disappointing some people who are counting on me to fit their vision of what a woman with Orthodox ordination should be. After all, opening up always includes exposing oneself, stripping oneself bare of those layers of protection. But it also opens one up to living wholly as oneself.

Should I insist on traditional halakhic guidelines in this service I was organizing in my home? Should I insist on a male prayer leader? Should I make sure there would be ten men present for a traditional male minyan? Or should I go with my heart, my intuition, which was telling me that applying these rules was totally inappropriate in this context?

To help me make these decisions, I decided to look at the traditional halakhic sources. There is no mention of women counting or not counting in a minyan, a prayer quorum of ten, in the Talmud. The only mention of this issue in the Talmud (Mishnah Megillah 4:3) requires that ten individuals be present in order to recite certain prayers, but there is no elaboration upon the sex of those individuals.[9] The first rabbinic sources to explicitly exclude women from being counted in a minyan are found in the Geonic and Medieval periods, although most halakhic

---

[9] A Canaanite slave is explicitly excluded, but a woman's status vis-à-vis minyan is not mentioned either way. One could say that it is understood that if a Canaanite slave is excluded, so is a woman, since their status in terms of religious ritual is usually the same. On the other hand, one could argue that since only the Canaanite slave is mentioned as excluded from counting in a minyan while the Mishnah is silent in regards to women, perhaps the author of this Mishnah could imagine women being counted under certain circumstances or at some point in time when women's status is different.

authorities of the time did not address the issue at all.[10] This position is later codified in the Shulkhan Aruch, written by Rabbi Yosef Karo in 16th century Israel.

Studying these sources this time around, I saw three ways to read this phenomenon. One was that the Mishnah could entertain the possibility that a woman could actually be included in the quorum of ten required for these prayers. After all, it does not say otherwise. But since women were not counted at that period in history in general in a public quorum, the rabbis left the issue open. In other words, in principle, they were not against the idea, but it was simply not their reality. When a woman is forbidden from a ritual act, this is made clear. So since it is not made clear here, perhaps that is because there is no essential thing about women that would exclude them forever from counting. It is simply because they were more akin to slaves (who were not counted) than free men at that point in history. But if women were to one day be more akin to free men than to slaves, perhaps they could be counted. So the Mishnah purposely left this option open.

Another way I saw to read this phenomenon was to say that in fact the Mishnah did not consider that a woman *could* be counted. Perhaps this was not an ideological decision not to include women. While the rabbinic scholars in this time period, the Tanaim, saw no halakhic reason to forbid women's inclusion, it simply did not occur to these rabbis to include women. In their time and place, a quorum meant ten free adult males, and no one questioned this definition. So the Mishnah does not even address the issue of counting women in a minyan.

A third possible reading is that the Tanaim considered it axiomatic that to include women in a minyan would be forbidden. And it is because it was so obvious to them that they did not even bother to write it.

According to the first two readings, it would follow that since there is no halakhic or ideological reason for women to be excluded from a minyan, in a time and place where it would actually seem natural to count them (which is my reality), we should count women. According to the third reading, I would argue that since no Talmudic source actu-

---

[10] See the *Siddur of Rav Saadya Gaon* in his commentary after *Yishtabach*; Rambam's *Mishneh Torah*, Laws of Prayer 12:3; Tosafot on BT Berachot 45b; and Meiri's *Beit Habechira* on BT Berachot 47b.

ally spells out women's exclusion, and since it is just as natural today for women to be counted as it was in Medieval times for women not to be counted, we should begin including women in the quorum of ten in those communities where such a step would be appropriate. It is likely that those Medieval rabbinic scholars added the word "males" because that was their cultural assumption. And in that case, we can interpret the Mishnah as not excluding the possibility of counting women in a minyan, since that is our cultural assumption.

These were sources I had studied and even taught for years. However, it was not until I was organizing this family service that I saw the necessity of my current conclusion. Until then, I had chosen to pray mostly in communities which did not count women in their minyan, and I had done so for two reasons. The first was that I did not see a way to get around the clear statement in the Shulkhan Aruch that ten males are required. The second was that I was not certain that total egalitarianism was the desired result of the movement seeking greater participation for women in synagogue services. I was trying to understand the wisdom of the Rabbis who saw a benefit in gender roles. Maybe it would not be so bad, I had thought, if women led certain prayers and men others, as long as women were permitted to lead some prayers. I thought it was wrong for women not to participate at all, but it was not important to me whether women were given complete access or only partial access.

In fact, I most preferred the model that allowed only women to lead those prayers that did not require a minyan and that were not an obligatory part of the service and only men to lead those prayers that did require a minyan and that were an obligatory part of the service. This presented an appearance of separate but equal, even if those educated in the intricacies of the halakhah were aware that in terms of obligation these prayers themselves were not actually "equal." Moreover, I liked the approach to minyan taken by one prayer community in which I was active. We waited until both ten men and ten women were present in order to recite the prayers for which a minyan is required. This seemed to me like a fine solution.

But that was before I had really listened to CHaNaH's voice. That was before I had come to the conclusion that playing by the rules of the patriarchy and preserving the status quo of distinct gender roles was not going to fix our broken world. Separate but equal is a lie. As long as we (men and women alike) are limited by our gender, we will never be able to fully realize our potential in this world, and we will never experience a world in which all voices are truly being heard and nothing is taken for granted. What had seemed unclear before was now as clear as the black-on-white letters of a Torah scroll: The distinctions that exist between men and women because of biological differences formed by God are all we need. The rest are oppressive, serving only to keep women from disturbing the patriarchy.

Was Moses' radiance from Torah alone? The light Moses received from the fire of Torah must have mixed with his inner Divine Light. I would read Rabbi Simeon ben Lakish to be saying that not only did Moses receive his radiance from a mixture of Torah and his own inner Divine Spark, but that the Torah itself was influenced by Moses' Divine Spark, and that this is a model for Torah in general. If we are all created in God's Image, if there is a spark of God in each of us, then Revelation is really an ongoing process that includes the input of each and every Divine Spark to be created. These are the sparks that we need to fix our broken world. After all, if Moses was simply a vessel for Torah, what would have been the purpose of choosing him to lead at all? Anyone could have done the job. Certainly God's reason for choosing Moses had something to do with his own personal narrative, his own strengths and weaknesses, his own intuition and moral conscience—what we call the spark of God that is found in each and every one of us.

The midrash tells us that when Moses finished writing the Torah, its fire illuminated his face. I believed so passionately in my current interpretation of the sources, that it felt to me like the fire of Torah itself. I felt the heat and light of this Torah connecting with the Divine Light inside of me, illuminating my own face. If I could bring this out, I would be increasing the light in the world, bringing us closer to eternal Shabbat.

The sources had not changed. But I had. Time and again, when I went through the families I had invited and thought of which people would be best suited for which roles, it was mostly the women who came to mind. In this particular group and context, traditional gender roles certainly did not apply. They were an anachronism.

Moreover, I felt that the decision was out of my hands at that point. It had been made for me. It was organic. It was natural, at least for this community. Not counting every adult present seemed absurd. The formal halakhah that excludes women from minyan felt totally inapplicable in this context, and the spirit of what a minyan is all about was telling me we undoubtedly had a minyan. With ten capable free adult agents, all equal in the eyes of God, how could we not recite those prayers required when a minyan is present? It felt like an affront to God's name not to recite them.

This was a turning point for me. I had worked through the sources and the sociological ramifications. I had spent years working out the halakhic issues and taking the step-by-step route of introducing women's participation in order to remain within the Orthodox community and play by the rules of the male-created halakhic system. But I couldn't play that game anymore. I suddenly felt free of those constraints. I felt empowered to go against the word of the Shulkhan Aruch in this case, despite the fact that the rest of the liberal Orthodox community did not seem similarly empowered.

I decided that I would listen to the voices of the rabbis before me and incorporate them into my decision-making process, but I would not let those voices be the final word. I was reminded of a term coined by Rachel Adler: "a halakhah." Adler is radical as a Reform theologian in her advocacy of a system of action that embodies what she considers modern Jewish ethics, but she calls this system "a halakhah" to differentiate it from traditional Orthodox halakhah that she refers to as "the halakhah."[11] Suddenly I understood her idea of "a halakhah" to be about incorporating Chanah's voice into the system at least as equally as the voices of the Rabbis. As Mordechai Kaplan, the founder of Reconstructionist Judaism had said years before: "Tradition has a vote, but not a veto." Somewhere in the halakhic process, my voice had to be heard. Chanah's voice had to be heard. So I listened to these voices and then to my inner voice, to Chanah's voice, and I let that be my guide.

---

[11] Adler, Rachel. *Engendering Judaism: An Inclusive Theology and Ethics* (JPS, 1998), p. 21

At my "Family Minyan" a woman led Shacharit, and the roof did not fall in.

We did not have ten men present, but we did have ten adults, and there was no doubt in my mind that these ten adults honored the Holy Presence in my home that had become a space to receive God's light that Shabbat; so we recited those prayers only recited in the presence of a minyan ("*dvarim shebikdusha*"), and despite the rain storm raging outside, lightning did not strike.

> "And the daughters of Tzelofchad drew near" (Numbers
> 27:1). When Tzelofchad's daughters heard that the land would
> be divided according to the tribes—to the males and not the
> females—they gathered together for advice.
>
> They said: "The Goodness of God is not like the good-
> ness of flesh and blood. Flesh and blood show greater
> goodness to males than to females. But the One-Who-
> Spoke-the-World-into-Being is not so, but is good to
> all. As it says, 'The Lord is good to all and shows kindness to all
> creatures'" (Psalms 145:9).
>
> —Sifre Bamidbar 133

This morning I was at the Western Wall, the Kotel, praying with Women of the Wall, a women-only prayer group that has been meeting monthly on the New Moon in the women's section of the Kotel for the past fifteen years. It is Rosh Chodesh Tevet, the New Moon that always falls on Chanukkah. One core member of our group had just returned from a few weeks in the States, where she went to say goodbye to her mother who was dying of cancer. Now she is in mourning, trying to recite the mourner's Kaddish at least once a day with a minyan.

Since the "Family Service" I held in my home, I had been thinking about whether ten women should be considered a minyan. If they were, women could recite the minyan-only prayers in women-only prayer groups. At the prayer service in my home, I had come to the conclusion that in the social frameworks in which I pray, it is absurd not to count the women along with the men. The idea of a minyan is that ten Jews praying together have the power to bring the Shechina, the earthly presence of God. Is it possible that only ten men have this power? I had already decided for the service in my home that a mixed group of men and women have this power. What of a group of only women?

The presence of the Shechina was potent as we completed the Hallel prayer this morning at the Kotel. I began to see clearly the right thing to do. When it was time for the mourner's Kaddish, my friend and I both turned to each other, and I said: "I think you should say Kaddish for your mother."

With tears in her eyes, she answered: "I was thinking the same thing."

And so, we announced to the group what was about to happen, and my friend said Kaddish for her mother at the Kotel. It was a powerful moment: the first time a woman had recited Kaddish with this group. This woman, who had been with the group for close to fifteen years, had, in my mind and in hers, earned the right to say Kaddish for her mother at the Kotel on Rosh Chodesh. She had been praying there each Rosh Chodesh morning—rain or shine—for all those years, lugging the Torah there in a duffel bag most of those mornings, since the Torah scroll is kept in her home. The Kotel was just as much hers as any male Jew who frequented it.

And her mother, who had prayed with us when she visited Israel, would have wanted it that way. A woman who was active in her egalitarian synagogue in the U.S. and a strong supporter of women's rights, she would have been proud to have her daughter recite the mourner's Kaddish for her at the Kotel. In fact, in my mind, her mother had also earned this Kaddish.

Rabbi Nachman says: When listening to women, you discover the Shechina.

Rabbi Nachman was no feminist. Certainly not in any contemporary use of the term. He did not think highly of women. He says that their intellectual capacity is low, and that men should give them respect precisely because of this fact. In other words, women are not deserving of respect, but they are in need of it. Like children.

And so, it is fascinating to hear from him that by listening to women, you can tap into the Shechina. Perhaps for Rabbi Nachman, God awareness has nothing to do with intellect. Perhaps for him, thinking can get in the way of truly knowing God. Ironically, Rabbi Nachman saw himself as the most intellectually capable of all. Yet he was the *tzadik*, the Rebbe, the one most tuned into God.

Perhaps Rabbi Nachman felt both ways of tapping into God's Will are necessary to achieve complete God awareness. What he would have called the male way of tuning-in to God is caught up in the intellect, in text study and analysis. Women's connection to God, he seems to be saying, is instinctual. Perhaps Rabbi Nachman felt he had both abilities of tuning in.

I am not prepared to accept Rabbi Nachman's gender assessments. Moreover, I refute essentialist arguments about gender. Yet, he lived in the 18th century when women were much less familiar with Jewish texts, and so I can forgive him his misogyny and chauvinism. But his insight about women's innate closeness to God fascinates me because he seems to recognize that a purely intellectual approach to tuning in to God misses something.

So, if feminism is going to change Judaism, perhaps this is one of the ways. If feminism is about revolution, challenging the status quo, and dissolving hierarchy, then incorporating this marginalized voice should be part of what this revolution is all about. Even if I am not willing to say that this is the way women essentially relate to God, it is certainly true that Judaism has been dominated by men and the male perspective and the male interpretation of God's Revelation until this point in our history. It is also true that much of this interpretive mode has been through the intellect, through text study and analysis.

Bringing in Chanah's voice will mean opening ourselves to additional ways of getting closer to God. The voice that tells us that something has gone amiss in the strictly textual analytical approach to interpreting God's Will cannot be silenced or marginalized any longer. Call it an instinctual antenna to the Divine, if you will. But this is the voice that tells us something is not right in the current system. The current system has not succeeded in sufficiently interpreting God's words. Not only is strict religious adherence not helping to solve our most urgent human crises, but often it is part of the problem. People are suffering and hurting others in the name of religion.

People follow the halakhah like sleepwalkers, as Rabbi Nachman himself puts it. They are not succeeding in waking up in awe of the Divine and they are not engaged enough—or in an appropriately directed way—in the process of repairing our broken world. Something is not right. There is a need for improvement. The time has come to listen to that voice, once suppressed, that can bring us closer to the Shechina and to the Divine Will.

> *Rav Aha said, Israel is likened to an olive tree: "A leafy olive tree fair with goodly fruit (Jeremiah 11:16)." And the Holy One is likened to a lamp: "The lamp of the Lord is the spirit of man (Proverbs 20:27)." What use is made of olive oil? It is put into a lamp, and then the two together give light as though they were one. Hence, the Holy One will say to Israel: My children, since My light is your light and your light is My light, let us go together—you and I—and give light to Zion: "Arise, give light, for thy light has come (Isaiah 60:1)."*
> — Sifre Bamidbar 133

In the Kiddush we recite over the wine on Friday nights, we say that Shabbat is a reminder of the Exodus from Egypt. What is the connection? When the Israelites were enslaved in Egypt, there was no marking of time. Time was one long endless stream. They had no holidays and no Shabbat. Being enslaved can mean having no rhythm, no structure, no base from which to grow. And thus, being free can sometimes mean choosing to remain grounded within a framework. But this can only work when the framework is truly self-imposed, because when it is forced upon the self, even subconsciously, from the outside, then this is no longer freedom. It is bondage.

So what does it mean to be free to serve God? God took us out of Egypt for this purpose. But with a whole set of rules that were created by the Rabbis as to how to serve God, how can we know when we are truly freely serving God? And how can we know when we are truly choosing our framework or when we are buying into a system that in some ways liberates us but in other ways oppresses us? Maybe the answer is to allow ourselves the freedom to critique the rabbis who came before us, to consider their wisdom and learn from it but not accept it as the final word. But can there be grounding without bowing to authority? Will too much autonomy lead to anarchy? Will personalized religious practice and decision-making lead to the end of Torah and Judaism?

In a previous point in our history, perhaps. When the Israelites left Egypt, they might not have been ready or suited for this kind of freedom or complexity. They were just slaves in Egypt, with no autonomy at all. So much autonomy all at once may have been too much for them to handle. And so, when they were offered the Torah at Mt. Sinai, they answered "*naaseh vinishmah*, we will do and then we will listen." In order to be free, they had to submit to God's Will. They needed a Master of some kind. Not a human master, but a Divine Master. That was the step they were ready to take at that time.

Moreover, in their case, they were hearing directly from God. The laws we are expected to follow today are interpretations by only male rabbis of what the Israelites heard directly from God. Our situation is more complex. It leaves more room for doubt, but it also leaves more room for personal investment and participation in what was meant to be an ongoing process of interpreting God's Will.

Today we need to listen first. Today, total submission does not mean freedom. Today, partnership is the more appropriate model: a three-way partnership, between God, the classical rabbis, and the Divine Light in each of us. We need the olive oil and the lamp in order to reach that ultimate light Isaiah speaks of. Life has become too complex for a theological approach of total submission. But this does not mean that we don't want the laws. We too want to accept the Torah. Our answer is just different: "*Nishmah vina'aseh*, we will listen and then we will do." In our reality, this is the only way to be free.

This February Shabbat we are at the Dead Sea. A field school at Ein Gedi, to be exact. In order not to miss my daily swim, I have researched swimming options in the area (the Dead Sea is so salty one cannot swim in it, only float on the surface of the water). There is an indoor lap swimming pool at Kibbutz Ein Gedi, which is two kilometers from the field school. After praying in the morning, I set out on foot to the kibbutz. I tell Jacob that I will meet him and the kids at Nachal David, a beautiful hike with natural springs and breathtaking views of the desert, which is next door to the field school.

I am not sure how long the walk will take me, but I set out grateful to have some time to myself. Everything around me is still and silent; I feel like the only human being on earth. There is not a ripple in the waters of the Dead Sea, and no cars on the road. No people. I don't even see birds or other wildlife. At the field school, there are herds of ibex constantly grazing, but here there is nothing. No one. Just me, the sky, the water, and the road ahead.

I am reminded of a Shabbat the summer before when Meira and I were hiking on the top of Ajax Mountain while on vacation in Aspen, Colorado. There too it was totally silent, and we were completely alone. The world looked still: Shabbat at its best.

The irony was that I doubted that any halakhic authority today would have approved of this choice of a Shabbat activity. Since the gondola that took us to the top of the mountain operates non-stop, all day, and since the condominium we were renting for the month was only a few blocks away from the gondola, I decided it was okay for a Sabbath observer to hop on and get a ride. And we had already purchased a monthly pass for the gondola. But I had no illusions that taking the gondola up the mountain would be considered in the spirit of Shabbat to a more traditional

Sabbath observer than me. Nevertheless, I had come to the conclusion that what is or is not in the spirit of Shabbat is relative. The idea of being on top of the highest mountain in Aspen on Shabbat felt so very "*Shabbosdik*" to me. For me, being there on top of that mountain on a Shabbat afternoon realized *oneg Shabbat*, a pleasurable Sabbath.

As we hiked atop Ajax Mountain, Meira and I talked about Shabbat and its meaning. She said that hiking on top of that mountain did not feel like Shabbat to her. I said it felt very much like Shabbat to me. She justified her view by noting that we didn't go to shul—although we did pray back in our condominium that morning, what my kids call "making a shul in our house" —and do the things she was used to doing on Shabbat in Jerusalem. I understood her point. For her, Shabbat meant going to synagogue and being part of a Shabbat community; but for me, Shabbat can be experienced in a variety of ways. In fact, if on Shabbat I am always with community—especially if that means being inside all day, either in synagogue or sitting around a table—I feel stifled and claustrophobic. I appreciate some quiet, alone, meditative time on Shabbat—especially if it includes being outdoors. So for me, being on top of Ajax Mountain on Shabbat was a rare opportunity for me to experience Shabbat in that way I often feel missing in my life. This does not mean that I would want to spend every Shabbat in this way. I also appreciate the feeling of gathering with others in shul on Shabbat—to pray together, check in with one another, and feel the warmth and support of community. But for me to be able to give to and benefit from community, I also need time to commune with my Sabbath soul.

"I can feel the world resting," is how I described it to Meira that summer day. Which is exactly how I feel now, walking along the Dead Sea on this winter Shabbat day.

I walk slowly, since my weakened leg muscles don't let me walk faster. In the end, the walk takes me much longer than I anticipated, because of my slow speed and the fact that there is a long climb up from the road to the kibbutz. And then once I am at the kibbutz, finding the swimming pool is another challenge. By the time I set off to meet Jacob and the kids, it is much later than we planned.

As I am walking, a man stops his car. "Do you want a lift?" he asks

me in Hebrew, albeit with an Arabic accent, so I know he is not Jewish. I
consider taking him up on his offer. It is late, and Jacob and the kids may
be worried about me. The man is driving anyway; he wouldn't be driving
for me, and he is not Jewish, so he is not violating the traditional halakhot of Sabbath observance. And I am far from home and my community,
so I feel I have license to do things I may not do when part of a traditionally observant Sabbath community. On the other hand, for me, surrendering to time and nature is an essential part of Shabbat. Sure, there
may be easier and faster ways to get from place to place than setting out
on foot; but totally entering into an experience in nature, not knowing
how long it will take, and knowing that there is no way you can control
the situation, seems to me to be very much what Shabbat is about.

I am reminded of a children's book: *Henry Hikes to Fitchburg*, by D.B.
Johnson, which is based on a quote from 19th century naturalist Henry
David Thoreau in his famous book, *Walden*:

> One says to me, "I wonder that you do not lay up money; you
> love to travel; you might take the cars and go to Fitchburg today
> and see the country." But I am wiser than that. I have learned
> that the swiftest traveler is he that goes afoot. I say to my friend,
> "Suppose we try to see who will get there first. The distance is
> thirty miles; the fare ninety cents... Well, I start now on foot,
> and get there before night; ... You will in the meanwhile have
> earned your fare, and arrive there some time tomorrow, or pos-
> sibly this evening, if you are lucky enough to get a job in sea-
> son. Instead of going to Fitchburg, you will be working here the
> greater part of the day."

In *Henry Hikes to Fitchburg*, two bears, who dress and act like humans,
make a bet as to who can get first to Fitchburg. One unnamed bear (who
is referred to as "Henry's friend" throughout the book) says he will work
to earn the money to buy train fare, and the other bear, Henry, modeled after Thoreau, sets off on foot. In the end, Henry's friend arrives in
Fitchburg first, but that is only because Henry made so many enjoyable
stops along the way—making a raft and paddling up the Nashua River,

swimming in a pond, picking blackberries—while his friend worked hard to earn his fare.

I think of Henry David Thoreau when I tell the driver in Hebrew: "I'd rather walk, thank you."

Swimming is sacred to me. That I know. But what does that mean? Where does God fit into the picture?

In the Talmud, on page 15b in Tractate Shabbat, there is a discussion about whether or not one may rip clothing on Shabbat. First, the Gemara deals with the issue raised in the Mishnah of ripping upon learning of the death of a relative. The problem is that ripping in a constructive way—e.g. ripping a hole for a head in a cloth that would in effect turn the cloth into a shirt—is prohibited on Shabbat. Ripping in a destructive way—e.g. ripping in order to ruin a garment—on the other hand, is permitted. Is ripping upon hearing of a death constructive or destructive? It would seem that it is the latter, since the purpose is to ruin the garment. But since it is a mitzvah to rip one's garment upon hearing the news of the death of a relative or teacher, this kind of ripping is actually considered by the Rabbis to be constructive. And so, it seems that one could perform a mitzvah while violating a Sabbath prohibition.

Then the Gemara turns to the issue brought up in the Mishnah of ripping as an expression of anger. Is this destructive or constructive ripping? Upon first glance, one would think that it is destructive. But the Gemara brings the opinion of Rabbi Abin that ripping in anger is constructive. He bases this on the saying of Rabbi Yochanan ben Guri that ripping in anger feeds the *yetzer harah* because expressing anger is giving in to one's evil inclination. In fact, it may lead to idol worship. One day the *yetzer harah* may say to give in to your anger, and the next day it may say to do something else, until you end up worshiping idols, *avodah zarah*.

This discussion in the Gemara speaks directly to my internal struggle regarding swimming on Shabbat. On one hand, I could understand swimming on Shabbat as feeding my evil inclination. Like ripping in anger, it is not a terrible infraction. In fact, it can even be seen as positive.

After all, if you rip in anger, perhaps you won't strike a human being. And if I swim on Shabbat, my enjoyment of Shabbat and my general health will be enhanced.

The question is: Is it my *yetzer harah* that is convincing me that this is so? Perhaps, as Rabbi Yochanan ben Guri suggests, such small concessions to the evil inclination will lead to larger ones, and not just any larger one, but the particular sin of idol worship. His choice of sin here is not incidental. I think he is implying that convincing ourselves that what we are doing is fine, even beneficial, when we know deep down inside that it is not really what God wants for us, is worshiping something other than God. Whether it be worshiping the thing itself, or whether it be worshiping ourselves, the problem is that God is no longer the highest power.

According to one midrash,[12] even the holy task of building the Tabernacle had to be interrupted for Shabbat. If the Israelites had not been made aware of this, they might have worshiped the Tabernacle itself rather than seeing it as a vessel of holiness, a path towards a greater communion with the Divine but not the Divine itself.

Perhaps the very thing that made the Tabernacle so holy was that it was not built on Shabbat. It was a holy object because it was built in full awareness of the fact that there is something yet holier. The Tabernacle never became the be-all and end-all, because the people had to stop working on it every six days. They were constantly reminded that their building was less important than the One who would ultimately dwell in it. In this sense, the Tabernacle stands in direct contrast to the Golden Calf, because the Golden Calf was built in an uninterrupted frenzy of excitement. The people gathered together, pooled their gold, threw it into the fire, and out came the Calf. If Shabbat fell out in the middle of this process, the people surely would not have noticed, as they were far too consumed by their ecstasy.

In this way, swimming seven days a week could become idol worship. Not because of any halakhic violations that might be involved; rather, it can become idol worship in the sense that it means that swimming is something that knows no bounds. It is an addiction, a dependence on

---

[12] See Rashi's commentary on Exodus 31:13.

something outside of myself that I imbue with a false sense of power. If I swim every day of the week, then the activity is not at all restrained in a way that makes for holiness. Choosing not to swim on Shabbat could be a form of restraint that could infuse my swimming on all other days with a sense of holiness.[13]

Part of me is drawn to this approach, but the other part of me, the part that struggles with authority, refuses to go along. It is the Rabbis, and not God, who issued an edict against swimming on Shabbat, and they did so in a specific time and place with a specific population in mind. And while it is important for us to give a tremendous amount of weight to traditional interpretations, it seems to me that considering these interpretations the eternal word of God would also be akin to idol worship. Imbuing this man-made system with a false sense of power and following it blindly to the point of dependence and a loss of self can itself be an addiction.

There is a danger of making an idol out of Torah. Torah is how God communicates with us, but Torah is not God. While God may be eternal and unchanging, Torah is eternal but forever in flux. Idols are stagnant, rigid. They cannot change or adapt with time. But Torah can. That is what keeps it alive. Therefore, as the world changes, our interpretations of Torah must change along with it. Swimming today is a pleasure. It is not associated with bathing, boating, cooking, or laundry. It is pure delight, *oneg*. And so, I see no reason to prevent any individual or community who experience swimming as *oneg* and as within the spirit of the Sabbath, from swimming on Shabbat. Similarly, someone whose Sabbath soul suffers from sitting in synagogue all Shabbat morning should take a walk instead.

It all comes back to the Sabbath: Shabbat as transcendent, but here, in this world. If Shabbat is a taste of the World to Come, then we strive for Shabbat as we work to repair this broken world. But is it realistic to strive for a Day that is All Shabbat while living in this World? Perhaps we need *chol*—the reality of our life in this World—to balance that out and keep us grounded in reality. Perhaps that is why letting go of all controls, comforts, and compromises that make us able to function and

---

[13] Thank you to Ilana Kurshan for these thoughts.

take pleasure in this world would be a mistake—even if only for one day each week. Since such a day would not be pleasurable for me, it would mean compromising my *oneg Shabbat*. The Rabbis had this very tension in mind when they introduced the principle of *oneg Shabbat* to balance out ascetic tendencies—such as sitting in the dark—that they felt were inappropriate for a day of rest for humanity.

The Rabbis themselves recognized the tension between earthly pleasures (*oneg*) and spiritual pursuits. And they recognized both as vital for a complete Sabbath experience. And both of these poles are represented in the candle lighting ritual. For me, Shabbat without swimming is how the Rabbis imagined Shabbat without light. They made candle lighting a mitzvah for this reason. After all, the Torah tells us not to kindle a fire on Shabbat. The Rabbis could have interpreted this to mean that fire, light, is forbidden on Shabbat all together. But for them, a day without light was antithetical to their image of what an enjoyable day is like. They could not imagine pleasure without light. Because for me, swimming is the only way I can move with the ease and freedom most others experience even on land, a day without swimming is for me like a day without light must have seemed to the Rabbis.

Yet, I can also see the spiritual benefit in being able to let go on Shabbat of this need to swim. So, just as the Rabbis made a conscious decision not to forbid light on Shabbat because of how that would affect the enjoyment of the day, I am following in their conceptual model by permitting myself to swim on Shabbat. Nevertheless, if the Shabbat candles were to accidentally blow out in the middle of Shabbat dinner, the traditional halakhic approach would not be to relight them, but rather to go to a friend's home or finish the meal in the dark. This approach recognizes that Shabbat can best be enjoyed with light, but it also acknowledges the spiritual benefits of being able to improvise and even let go of the need for light when circumstances don't allow for it.

I am reminded of a Shabbat a few years ago when I went with my extended family to a hotel on the beach for my cousin's son's bar mitzvah. It was winter, and I knew there was no indoor swimming pool. Instead, I took a walk on the sea shore. The terrain was rugged, full of cliffs and rocks and dunes, so it was more of a hike than a walk, with the sound of waves crashing against the rocks as I hiked. The walk was not easy for me, and I knew my muscles would be tired later on, but I enjoyed it in the moment nonetheless, knowing that this was an exceptional Shabbat for me. The night before had been stormy, and when I set out on the hike, there was still a light rain falling. As I walked, the rain subsided, and the most magnificent rainbow appeared. It stretched across the entire sky and remained in view for at least half-an-hour. I was not at all sorry that I had gone away that Shabbat. Hiking on the sea shore and seeing the rainbow were compensation for my missed Shabbat swim.

Now I understand that I have to keep that memory part of my Shabbat theology. I must remember that there are other ways to experience the kind of spiritual and physical freedom that I feel when swimming, ways that may even surpass my swimming experience. Swimming is a way to ensure that experience, a safe way to be certain that I will have that *oneg Shabbat* feeling. But swimming cannot be the only way, because if it is, it becomes *avodah zarah*; it becomes an addiction. Swimming is only a safe vehicle for this world, a sure-fire way to taste Shabbat even on a week-day, but it is not the essence itself. It is not Shabbat, because Shabbat is the taste of another world.

On Shabbat, I must let go of my need for safety and control and open myself to experience the essence itself. But only in a way that feels safe to me in my own reality, since in the end, I inhabit this world, not the World to Come. Worries, illnesses, sorrow, and tragedy like calories do not magically disappear on Shabbat. And so, we do need to "work" to make our Sabbath day a pleasure. Some of us more than others. And for me, at least, letting go of my Shabbat swim would be breaking a personal boundary instead of expanding it. My search for my Sabbath soul has helped me understand that.

This journey to connect to my Sabbath soul has also helped me understand that full egalitarianism expands my boundaries and does not break them.

God gave our ancestor Jacob an additional name when he became the father of the Jewish nation: *Yis-ra-El*, He Who Wrestles with God. And so, my goal is to keep on wrestling. To keep on struggling with my own relationship with God and Torah and mitzvot and what it means to be Jewish. In other words, I am content with never being totally "cured," never being totally "whole," never reaching the spiritual heights that Nadav and Avihu reached, because I am human. I live with compromise, imperfection, and brokenness, and I am constantly balancing my many values, priorities and needs. And so, this is what I do as well when fashioning for myself a Shabbat experience and when helping others do the same for themselves.

So, for instance, when my friend asked me if she should drive to visit her in-laws on Shabbat for their family's regular monthly Friday night Shabbat gatherings, I told her first that it was her decision to make. My general approach when asked a halakhic question is to make it clear that I am not giving a halakhic ruling, since I believe that each person must decide for him or herself how to live a Jewish life and take responsibility for this decision. I am happy to share my knowledge and guidance, but I will not make the final decision. Moreover, I now understand that there is no one correct answer to a halakhic question, and there is no one single correct definition of Shabbat. Each person must get in touch with his or her own personal Shabbat soul.

After I made this clear, I told her that driving to these family Friday night gatherings seemed reasonable considering her imperfect situation. If she stayed for all of Shabbat with her in-laws, who do not observe the Sabbath in the way she does, her children would not have what she considers a Shabbat experience the whole next day. But if they do not go at all, her children would never experience being part of that monthly family experience with their cousins and grandparents and uncles and aunts that is also a strong value for my friend. So, like me with my swimming, my friend was in a bind. Her Shabbat was lacking without driving to the family gatherings, but her Shabbat would also be lacking if she did drive. An imperfect situation in an imperfect world. But part of her job as a human-being-God-wrestler would be to decide what to do.

There was no way I could have programmed that rainbow over the beach into my day. I had no way of knowing that it would appear. But if I had not opened myself to that experience by letting go of my need to swim, I would never have seen that rainbow. And that is Shabbat in its most pure form: opening up to experience God's glory. Yet, that does not mean that I must approach every Sabbath this way. Since I know that not every Shabbat will bring a rainbow, I try to fashion a pleasurable Sabbath experience for myself by at least having my swim on a regular Shabbat. Then I know that my Shabbat will at least on some level be a day of *oneg*. And that is okay for some of the time. As long as I am able to let go of my daily swim when a real conflict occurs.

I have decided to allow myself that leeway—at least for now—as long as I constantly remind myself of the importance of opening my Shabbat soul to life's rainbows.

One morning during my weekly hevruta study of Rabbi Nachman of Breslov, I came to understand why the dissonance between ritual and meaning, between law and spirituality, was for me most symbolized by and manifest in Shabbat. My hevruta and I went on a tangent discussing the teachings of Rabbi Zalman Schachter-Shalomi, the founder of the Jewish Renewal movement, on "Paradigm Shift," especially in the context of Shabbat.[14]

According to Rabbi Schachter-Shalomi, Judaism evolves organically with cultural cosmic paradigms that change over time. Based on a Hasidic understanding of the Kabbalistic work Sefer Yetzirah, there are actually three stages Judaism must go through along with the rest of society in order to reach a repaired world. The first stage, or paradigm, was *Olam* (literally "world"), which ended roughly around the destruction of the Second Temple (the space where God was felt to be located). In other words, in that paradigm, it was in space where the Divine was felt to be located and locatable.

---

[14] This explanation of Rabbi Schachter-Shalomi's teachings about Paradigm Shift in Jewish religious development was based on an oral discussion I had with his student, Rabbi Ruth Gan Kagan. See chapter 5 in her book, *Jewish Renewal: Integrating Heart and World* (Yedioth Books, 2006). See also *Integral Halachah* (Trafford Publishing, 2007) by Daniel Segal and Zalman Schachter-Shalomi; Schachter-Shalomi's *Yishmru Daat: Chassidic Teachings of the Fourth Turning* (Albion-Andalus Books, 2013); *Paradigm Shift: From the Jewish Renewal Teachings of Rabbi Zalman Schachter-Shalomi* (Jason Aronson, 2000) by Ellen Singer; and *Jewish with Feeling: A Guide to Meaningful Jewish Practice* (Riverhead Trade, 2006) by Zalman Schachter-Shalomi and Joel Segal.

Shanah (literally "year") then took over as the dominant paradigm, which is when Shabbat, holidays and other time-oriented rituals became the locus of the Divine energy. Instead of Temple sacrifices, we offer our time up to God. Shabbat, which has been described by Rabbi Abraham Joshua Heschel as replacing the Temple with a sanctuary in time, is the best example of this. It is the day each week when we stop *doing* and instead simply *be*.

Rabbi Schachter-Shalomi maintains that we are now shifting away from that paradigm, into *Nefesh* (literally "soul"). According to Schachter-Shalomi, today it is not in Space or Time that we find the Divine, but rather inside of each and every one of God's creations. We are in the age of human rights, human dignity, and self-fulfillment, which is why certain Jewish concepts and practices that are either space- or time-oriented no longer work for us. When we practice them we experience dissonance. They are part of the paradigm which we are in the process of shifting out of.

If we accept this theology, the question is: Will we embrace the paradigm shift, or will we fight it? Will we find a way to adapt traditional Jewish concepts and practices to the new paradigm so they can continue to resonate, or will we let them become empty shells, piles of burnt rubble, devoid of meaning?

When the scholars in the Gemara say that the Mishna's 39 activities forbidden on Shabbat are based on the work involved in the Tabernacle, it seems clear that this is not a literally true statement. In fact, the Gemara itself proves this by pointing out where this seems particularly far-fetched. Nevertheless, the Gemara then goes through great pains to prove the connection to be actually real. And why is that?

The application of the notion of Paradigm Shift tells us that the old paradigm of Space (the Temple) was no longer working (in fact, there was no longer a Temple standing), and now it was Time (Shabbat) where we found God's presence. But we felt the need to connect it back to the old paradigm for continuity's sake—in order to make the transition from *Olam* to *Shanah* as smooth as possible. What the Rabbis in the Gemara were saying, even subconsciously, was that they found God in Shabbat, in Time, in the way that their ancestors before them found it in Space, in the Temple. According to Rabbi Schachter-Shalomi's approach, the Rabbis connected Shabbat to the Tabernacle as a way to allow for the shift to happen without too much dissonance and rupture.

What I realized as I discussed this theory with my study partner that morning was that I had been experiencing the tension between the *Shanah* paradigm and the *Nefesh* paradigm, and, understandably, it was in Shabbat, which is about creating holiness in time, where I felt this dissonance most strongly. After all, if Shabbat is about giving up our time to God, that means having to put aside our egos and personal needs for a larger connection to the Divine. But in a paradigm that is centered on the dignity and holy essence of the individual, Shabbat can be especially challenging. At least that is what I was experiencing. I did not feel able to put aside my own personal notion of *oneg Shabbat* in order to comply with the rabbinic notion of that concept; nor did I want to surrender my personal Sabbath experience for the communal norm.

Moreover, the idea of Shabbat being a day totally different from all other days and removed from the reality of my life, from the essence of who I am (which includes my coping mechanisms too), did not work for me. The idea may be noble, but the Sabbath construct of creating a time removed from the reality of my life, even if for just one day a week, did not resonate with me spiritually, and now I understood why. The notion of creating a Temple in Time clashed for me with the notion of there being a Divine Spark inside each individual. The *Nefesh* paradigm was coming in conflict with the *Shanah* paradigm, which was why I felt unable to relate to the classic rabbinic expression of Shabbat. This interpretation of Sabbath observance was asking me to submit my individuality to a degree that for me was problematic; and the idea that by sanctifying time I could manage to do this just did not work. Now I was able to understand that dissonance within a larger historical and conceptual context.

So now I understood the root of my spiritual angst, but how could I ride the paradigm shift successfully? How could I make Shabbat a meaningful Jewish practice for me without losing a sense of continuity with the past?

As Ruth and I discussed this, I realized that I had already been struggling with this challenge. My journey to discover my Shabbat soul helped me let go of halakhic and communal constraints that had been getting in the way of my experience of a meaningful Shabbat. It helped me realize that letting go of these constraints is part of what we all need to do in order to enter into the new paradigm successfully. By applying a personalized approach to halakhah to our Sabbath observance, we are doing what the Rabbis did when they connected Shabbat back to the Temple. As the Rabbis in the Talmud connected *Shanah* to *Olam*, I connected *Nefesh* to *Shanah*. On a more superficial level, a *Nefesh*-oriented understanding of Shabbat leaves more room for individual interpretation of what Sabbath enjoyment and rest means. On a deeper level, it places God inside the individual, not in a holy space or in a unit of time.

Shabbat is many things. It is a psychological and physical respite from our regular weekday activities and preoccupations. It is a day of rest, recreation, and relaxation. It is a chance to stop and make note of what we have accomplished and think ahead to where we want to be in the future. It is a window in time when we can connect to our most profound spiritual core and let go of those more earthly concepts like time and money that can often get in the way of living in a deeper, more essential way. It is a time when we can open ourselves to life's rainbows. Yet, to submit to the rabbinic understanding of Shabbat and *oneg Shabbat* (or anything else for that matter) when it goes against the grain of one's own personal understanding, is really an act of a previous paradigm. Being true to one's personal notion of the deeper meaning and purpose of Shabbat is the way we, in our current reality, can enter the new paradigm without losing Shabbat entirely.

The ritual act of lighting the Sabbath lamp was a revolutionary rabbinic creation that saved Shabbat in its time. It made it possible to both keep and enjoy the Sabbath. Today we must take similar courageous steps to save our Sabbath souls so that we do not lose the spiritual experience of Shabbat inside the morass of rules and regulations the Rabbis created for the day. When these rules get in the way of a spiritually restful experience, we need to be able to let go of them. Sometimes, having the courage to let go of tradition is what will save Judaism in the long run. The Rabbis of old knew this, and so they were able to shift into a new paradigm successfully in their time. Today we must follow their example. The Shabbat candles represent earthly pleasure, *oneg*, yet they also represent the Divine Spark that is inside each of us that is at the core of the *Nefesh* paradigm. Like Shabbat, that flame is where heaven (the Divine) and earth (humanity) meet.

"What we call the beginning is often the end. And to make an end is to make a beginning. The end is where we start from."
—T.S. Elliot

Pesach is a holiday of freedom, and this year, as this holiday approaches, I am working on freeing my soul to be itself. But this has not been an easy task. Just as the Israelites wandered for forty years in the desert before entering the Land of Canaan, I have been, and will continue to be, wandering, trying to find my way, before I can be totally free. But leaving Egypt, Mitzrayim, that narrow place, was perhaps the hardest step of all. Now the challenge is to find my way, taking one small step after another—and like the Israelites, having to trust that God will guide me.

Ten years ago, the rabbi I have been studying with for ordination told me that he would give me *smicha* when I felt ready. It has become clear that the time has come to go to him and tell him that I am ready. And so, I gather my courage and make an appointment. We have not discussed my desire for ordination recently, and I am worried that he may have changed his mind. I am pleasantly surprised that he has not. He tells me to write up a certificate that I think expresses what I have achieved on my road towards *smicha*, and what I wish to achieve in the future with my *smicha*, and bring it to him to sign.

Today, this is an unconventional way of receiving rabbinic ordination. But it may be closer to the traditional way this was done in the past, when getting *smicha* was a matter of your Rebbe telling you the time has come to leave the yeshiva and go out and make your mark. In my case, the burden of making that decision was on me, which actually makes the experience all the more organic. I have been feeling for months now that I am ready to move on. I have no intention of ending my learning. In fact, I feel now more than ever that I have so much more to learn.

While I certainly have not exhausted my study of halakhah, I also realize now that studying halakhah is only the beginning, the tip of the everlasting flame of what we call Torah. My journey into the three women's mitzvot, my effort to learn Chanah's secret and give her voice, has taught me that. What I am seeking in this visit to my teacher is closure on this chapter of my life, because that is what it feels like now—a chapter. I want to end this chapter so I can begin another.

After some revision, my teacher agrees to sign my ordination certificate. The day I have been working towards for more than ten years has finally come. I am filled with relief. This chapter of my life is over and I am now free to be led on whatever path my inner Divine Light illuminates for me. The date on the certificate is the 14th of Nissan, Erev Pesach, which is the day before the Jewish Exodus from Egypt. This is a fast day for first born sons in the Jewish tradition, because it was on this day that the Angel of Death "Passed them Over" during the 10th plague, the massacre of the first born Egyptian sons. God spared those first born sons in the homes of the Israelites who showed that they believed by sacrificing a lamb and smearing its blood on their door posts.

This is a serious day, a day of fear and faith, a day of excitement and anticipation, a day of openness and willingness. Therefore, this was an appropriate day to return to my teacher so he could help me complete this chapter in my life. I too am embarking on a journey into the unknown, a step that has taken a great deal of faith, a willingness to put myself into the hands of God and open myself up to vulnerability. I too am filled with fear, excitement and anticipation.

I am deeply afraid of what's in store. I am afraid of the future. I am afraid of myself. I am afraid of others. But I am not afraid of God. I will open myself to letting God's light shine through me.

It is a rainy Shabbat in August. We are visiting a friend in Switzerland.

It is my time to go to the mikveh, and Jacob and I are planning to immerse together in Lake Geneva, which is just a fifteen-minute walk from her house. This will also work well in terms of my lap swimming plans, since I will be able to swim before we immerse.

But we did not anticipate the stormy weather. As the rain continues to fall, my friend suggests that she and I go over to the local indoor swimming pool—an hour-long walk from her home—where she is a member and has free passes for guests. But this means leaving Jacob alone with the kids, stuck in the house for about four hours. It also means subjecting ourselves to a long walk in the pouring rain. So I decide to stick to my idea of swimming in the lake and hope for the best. I am proud of my rational decision-making and my ability to let go of my obsessive need to swim. As a result, everyone will be able to better enjoy the Shabbat.

As the day goes on, we wait for the weather to clear; and finally, at around 5 pm, it does. And so, we all set out—Jacob, me, our five kids, our friend, and her dog. When we arrive at the lake, I strip down to my bathing suit and jump in. The water is very cold and choppy from the day's storm. I am able to swim, but not in any relaxed or methodical way because of the waves and the chill of the water.

I swim for about twenty-five minutes and decide I have had enough. The swim has been invigorating, and the view gorgeous, but if I continue to swim for a full hour, the swimming will no longer be *oneg Shabbat*. It will be the swim of a woman addicted to swimming an hour a day, and since I am no longer such a woman, I swim back to shore.

"You're done already?" Jacob raises his eyebrows.

"Yup. I'm ready for mikveh. But I'm also freezing. Let's do it now, before I get out. I'm afraid if I get out, I won't be able to get back in."

My friend takes the kids over to a different part of the shore to give us some privacy, and Jacob enters the water. "It *is* freezing," he confirms, as I remove my suit in the water and hand it over to him.

When we finish immersing, we walk to join the others—shivering from the cold, with our arms wrapped around each other for warmth. "Sorry you didn't really get to swim," Jacob says.

"It's okay," I say. "It was my decision to skip the indoor pool. Besides, that was a memorable swim. And I'm glad I was able to be relaxed about the whole thing. That's new for me, you know."

We join the others on a wooden bench. I look out at the water, and that's when I see it: a beautiful rainbow stretched clear across the sky.

In the Book of the Zohar (Genesis 48b) we find an alternate understanding of the reason that the mitzvah of Shabbat candle lighting was given especially to women:

> "... *Shabbat* candles were given to Jewish women to light [because] the Tabernacle of Peace is the Supernal Mother of the world, and the souls, which are supernal Candles, reside within her. Thus, a [woman] should light the candles. By doing so, she stands in the stead [of the Tabernacle of Peace and brings down holy souls into the world in the form of lights].
>
> A woman should light the candles of Shabbat with a joyful heart and great concentration, because the supernal Glory is hers. It is a great merit to her to beget holy children who are the shining candles of Torah and Piety, and who will bring *shalom* [peace or wholeness] to the world."[15]

This anachronistic gendered text does not speak to me in its literal form. Yet, connecting the Sabbath lights to holy souls waiting to be born and bring us closer to a perfected world does speak to me. This image evokes for me the notion of needing each individual soul in its uniqueness—each unsilenced and sincere voice—in order to reach a world that is in its entirety Shabbat.

Now when I light the Sabbath candles, I also keep in mind that this ritual act exemplifies Jewish ritual innovation at its best. The Rabbis took an act that was actually forbidden according to a literal understanding of the Torah—using fire on the Sabbath—and turned it into a mitzvah.

---

[15] The text above is my own translation and interpretation. I take liberties with the text to glean from it an understanding of the mitzvah of Shabbat candle lighting that fits my own feminist sensibilities and my human centered theology of the *Nefesh* paradigm.

And they did so in order to save the Sabbath. This is what I visualize in my mind's eye as I circle the flames with my hands. This is what the ritual represents for me now so that I would not want to give it up.

I now experience Shabbat candle lighting—perhaps the most time-bound, *Shanah*-centered, mitzvah of all—as a reminder to myself that halakhah is not a set system of stagnant rules interpreted in the past for all times, but rather a continually changing embodiment of progressing Jewish values in a changing reality with an ultimate goal of transformation and redemption. Change is essential. When I close my eyes to meditate over the Sabbath candles, I now remind myself of the importance of bestowing dignity to each and every soul, each and every light, each and every human being on this earth. Then I can truly connect with this mitzvah in my humanity-focused, *Nefesh*-centered, reality.

I have come a the place in my spiritual journey where as much as I enjoy going to shul, I also enjoy staying at home, watching the candles burn. I have even created a new routine for myself when I am the one who lights the candles. I recite a short prayer that I composed which combines two prayers written by women. One was written in Yiddish a hundred or more years ago; the other was written in Ladino by a Turkish woman in 1920:

> *Creator of the Universe, since I have fulfilled the three mitzvot of challah,* nidah, *and* hadlakat ha-ner, *the three ChaNaH mitzvot, let these mitzvot be an advocate before You, that I should merit in my home a light of joy, blessings, and peace. Let these candles remind me to make my Shabbat personally pleasurable and enjoyable so that I can experience the true spirit of the mitzvah of Shabbat. May You brighten our Shabbat souls with the splendor of Your Heavenly Presence and give us strength to tap into the Divine Spark with which you have blessed each and every one of us, and the courage to use that spark to ignite other holy fires.*
>
> Baruch Atah Adonai Aloheinu Melekh Haolam, asher kidishanu bimitzvotav vitzivanu lihadlik ner shel Shabbat. *Praised are You, Source of Life, Spirit of the Universe, Who*

sanctified us with the mitzvot and commanded us to kindle the
Sabbath lamp.

Rabbi Yeshayahu Horovitz, who lived in the 16th and 17th centuries in Eastern Europe, records the custom of women following the lighting of the Shabbat candles with a recitation of the prayer that Chanah recited in praise of and thanks to God after her son, the prophet Shmuel, was born. This custom seems to me appropriate—a *tikkun*, a corrective of the silencing of women that has been the Jewish model for so long. Chanah is traditionally seen as the model of how Jewish women should pray because she moved her lips without letting her voice come through. By reviving this empowering tradition of honoring Chanah's voice rather than her silence, we can begin to finally allow CHaNaH's voice—and with it the voices of Jewish women past, present and future—to be heard, to be part of the project of letting our individual Divine Lights illuminate Torah.

Moreover, it is due to another, later Chanah, Rashi's granddaughter, that we have preserved the women's tradition of first lighting the Shabbat candles and then reciting the blessing over them. It was rare for women to influence Jewish Law in that time period. And so, each time I now light Shabbat candles, I focus on that precedent for women's involvement in ritual and halakhic development. The fact that her name was Chanah strikes me as a significant sign of hope for the future as well. A line of Chanahs influencing Jewish ritual.

There is also the obvious connection between the name Chanah and the three women's mitzvot: **ch**allah, *nidah*, and *hadlakat ha-ner: CHaNaH*. My journey through the three CHaNaH mitzvot has helped me learn Chanah's secret of praying from her heart so I could give Chanah voice—by tapping into my own Divine Spark and allowing my inner voice to be heard. Perhaps the recording of my journey through the "CHaNaH" mitzvot will have its impact as well, following in the footsteps of these two significant Chanahs.

Yet while I want to hear and echo Chanah's voice, her prayer itself does not reflect my own inner voice. It is too triumphant, too gloating, and too sure of the inevitable fall of evildoers. Instead, I allude to Chanah's prayer with a line I adapted from the Prophet Zechariah (7:6), who expanded on a line from Chanah; it is because of what I learned on this journey that I can now stand before the Shabbat candles and recite this line:

Not by strength and law alone shall humans prevail, but also with compassion and spirit, heart and soul.

Then, based on a line found in a manuscript from Italy of a Shabbat candle-lighting prayer, I add:

The One who answered Chanah's prayer shall, please, answer mine.

As I stand lighting the Sabbath candles as my women ancestors did before me, I feel confident that their prayers and Chanah's prayers and my prayers are in some cosmic and very deep way one and the same. They have given me the ability to open myself up to and grow to cherish a whole world of transformative ritual that I once devalued as feminine. I have given Chanah and other powerful-in-their own-ways Jewish women throughout the centuries a voice. The voice of the Divine Spark that was inside them all along and is inside all of us—men and women alike—as well.

Amen.

AIR

Epilogue

Once we have left the waters of the womb, we have to construct a space for ourselves in the air for the rest of our time on earth... To construct and inhabit our airy space is essential. It is the space of bodily autonomy, of free breath, free speech and song, of performing on the stage of life.
— Luce Iragaray, *Sexes and Genealogies*

I AM STANDING OUTSIDE in my friend's garden, beneath a dark, hazy sky, surrounded by grape vines, fig, olive, date and pomegranate trees. This is a Garden of Eden in the city of Jerusalem. I am here with friends, men and women alike. We gathered here, one by one, as the sky grew dark and Shabbat left us, to recite the prayer for the New Moon: *Kiddush Levanah*.

There is a strong tradition of women refraining from saying this prayer that is traditionally recited on the first Saturday night of each month. In fact, to this day it is rare to see women reciting *Kiddush Levanah*. The prayer is not even included in The New Artscroll Women's Siddur, an Orthodox prayer book which came out in the year 2005. According to Rabbi Isaiah Horowitz—the same 16th century kabbalist and scholar who records the tradition of women reciting Chanah's prayer after lighting the Shabbat candles—women do not recite *Kiddush Levanah* because of their shame, for it was Eve, the first and archetypal woman, who caused the "blemish" to the moon. The Babylonian Talmud (Tractate Hulin 60a) relates that the moon and the sun were once of equal brilliance. But the moon complained that "two rulers cannot wear one crown," so God ordered her to make herself smaller.

According to Rabbi Horowitz, this shrinking of the moon, the imperfection in the world, at its root was caused by Eve's introduction of sin into the human narrative. She listened to her evil inclination, and because of this, the world is now imperfect. We were exiled from paradise, the Garden of Eden where there was no sin, and sent out into the world outside of the Garden where good and evil both exist. This was all because of Eve—because of women.

But the picture is more complex than that. Later on, at the incident of the Golden Calf, tradition has it that the women ignored their evil inclinations and did not join in the sin. According to one midrash (Pirke d'Rabbi Eliezer, chapter 45), they were rewarded with the celebration of

Rosh Chodesh, the New Moon, for not having participated in the sin of the Golden Calf. Women redeemed themselves, at least on some level, and so we were given this gift. Yet, Rabbi Horowitz says, we women are still too ashamed to come out and bless the New Moon, since we did cause its blemished state, after all. Even if we are helping to remedy the situation, even if we are working to fight off our evil inclinations, we were the ones who invited the evil inclination into the world in the first place!

The Jerusalem Talmud (Tractate Shabbat, chapter 2, page 5, column 2) provides a similar explanation for why women were given the three women's mitzvot of challah, nidah, and hadlakat ha-ner: Because Eve caused Adam's death and brought mortality into the world, women must make up for this by performing these three mitzvot, each of which is symbolic of Adam's death in some way. Says the Talmud: "The first Adam was the blood of the world... And Eve caused his death; therefore the commandment of menstrual separation was given to the woman. Adam was the first pure dough-offering of the world... And Eve caused his death; therefore she was given the commandment of the dough-offering. Adam was the candle of the world, for it says, 'the soul of Adam is the candle of God,' and Eve caused his death; therefore, the commandment of lighting the candle was given to the woman."

After studying these sources, I decided to personally take on the practice of reciting *Kiddush Levanah* each month.

The way I read it, the midrash that tells the story of the moon's diminishment is actually an attempt to tell the story of the creation of patriarchy, hierarchy, oppression, and hegemony in the world. The midrash places the blame for her diminished state on the moon herself. After all, she complained about having to share the reign. In other words, according to this midrash, those who are oppressed are guilty for their own oppression, their own lack of power.

But the blame is not completely on the moon. It was God who told her to make herself smaller. The fact that the midrash and Rabbi Horowitz put the blame for the imperfection of the world and humanity completely on women is twisted logic. It's blaming the victim, and blaming the powerless. Women are not the ones (or at least not the only ones) who brought the world to its present disastrous state where might is right.

Are we really to believe that we are ashamed to face the moon because it reminds us of our own guilt in creating our own oppression?

I think rather that men were afraid of what might happen were we to pray by the light of the moon for its restoration to its original grandeur. We might be reminded of our connection to the moon. We might be reminded of what the moon symbolizes for us: muted power, fuzzier lines, shared light. We might also be reminded of God's promise in Isaiah 30:26, which is referred to in the prayer of *Kiddush Levanah*, the promise that one day God will renew the moon and make the two lights equal in power. I think this idea scared the men in power, and so they discouraged women from reciting this prayer, as they discouraged our involvement with various other mitzvot that could interfere with men's religious expression and threaten men's ultimate control over women and society in general.

And for the mitzvot that were unavoidably the domain of women—challah, *nidah*, and *hadlakat ha-ner*—the fear of losing power took another form. Since women were the ones who baked the bread, experienced a cycle of fertility, and were in the home when it was time to light Shabbat candles, men had to trust women to perform these mitzvot properly. But this terrified them, since if the women did not perform them meticulously, the men too would be stricken with such severe punishments as death at the hands of God or being cut off from the Nation. Thus, the need to threaten women to be extremely scrupulous lest "they die in childbirth."

Kiddush Levanah is traditionally recited in a group. With my new-found understanding of the origin of women's distancing from the prayer, I organized a group of women to recite it with me each month. This went on for about six months. Then, a friend who had become a co-organizer of this group asked if I would mind if we opened the group to men. I thought about this and decided that it was a great idea. After all, the moon's imperfection symbolized for the Rabbis the general imperfect nature of the world. Restoring the moon to its former glory is symbolic of a general fixing of the world.

When we ate from the Tree of Knowledge and chose to be partners with God in ongoing Creation, we became, like God, in need of Shabbat. We too needed to learn to rest from the exhausting work of trying to fix our imperfect world, of trying to restore the moon to her former glory—to balance moon and sun, Shabbat and *chol*, *gevurah* and *hessed*, willfulness and willingness, and bring a certain wholeness that is missing now from the world. When we accomplish that, our work will be done, and we will have no more need for Shabbat, because life will be one long Shabbat. A transformed Shabbat. A Shabbat that incorporates and balances these two forces to the perfect measure so that it itself is transformed. A Day that is All Shabbat.

In order to reach that Day that is All Shabbat, we will have to figure out together how to share the crown. Renewing the moon means the end of the power struggle that, according to the midrash, caused the inequality of power that exists in the world in the first place. It means a transformed reality, the introduction of a new way of looking at the world. A renewal of the moon means women being transformed by men and men being transformed by women, and sun and moon in balance.

The first time we recited *Kiddush Levanah* as a mixed gender group, I felt validated in our decision to invite men. When we began, the moon was covered by a haze. We could see her just enough to recite the prayer, but barely. But when we came to the part of the prayer when we were meant to leap up and try to reach the moon, she started to shine through the haze. It was as if the light of the moon burned a hole in this curtain that was muting her radiance, and she became surrounded by a bright yellow halo, which expanded as we continued to dance and sing.

The moon was renewing herself before our eyes, but not in the usual monthly way. She was actually breaking through a barrier with her light, a reflection of the light of the sun. The two powers together broke through the haze that had clouded our vision. Together, their lights became a porthole to the Divine.

Afterword

AS THIS BOOK THAT I COMPLETED SEVEN YEARS AGO goes to press, I feel obliged to update my readers on some relevant developments in my life. I will relay them here in the order in which they occurred, not in order of importance:

First, Jacob has now become the official challah-baker in our house. When he announced that he was going to become a vegan, he also took upon himself the responsibility of making vegan challot for Shabbat each week. I did not believe vegan challot could be as tasty as my recipe, but Jacob proved my assumption wrong. However, his veganism is clearly not the only impetus for him to pull out the huge mixing bowl each Friday morning. Jacob has owned the act of baking challah. It has become a spiritual practice, and I am happy to have shared that experience with him. I assume that one day we will go back to sharing this mitzvah. But for now, I am giving Jacob the space to call this mitzvah his own.

Second, after the two miscarriages written about in this book, I suffered two more miscarriages and thus decided, along with Jacob, that it was best for us to channel our desire for a sixth child in another direction. It became clear to us that if we were indeed meant to have another child, it was going to have to happen in a less conventional way. Therefore, we applied to adopt a child. Eighteen months later, after many meetings with our social worker and a six-week required course in adoption parenting, we were blessed with our adoptive son, Mishael Adar Binyamin. He was five-and-a-half months old when he came to live with us, and his name was Binyamin. We added the other two names.

Mishael (which sounds like Moshe, the name of Jacob's late grandfather who died about a year before we adopted our son) means a request of God, which he truly was. And since Mishael joined our home in the month of Adar, a month with the theme of turning sadness into joy, we felt that was a suitable second name—especially since my Aunt Essie (short for Esther) passed away a couple of years before. Esther is the heroine of the Purim story, which falls in the month of Adar. We kept his given name, Binyamin, as a third name because it was not our intention to erase the first six months of his life.

Third, after running pre-marriage seminars and doing individual pre-marriage counseling for couples for a number of years, I was asked to officiate at the wedding of one of the couples I worked with. They wanted me because they wanted the wedding to be completely egalitarian. They didn't even want to exchange rings because of the financial-transaction-overtones of that ritual act. Everything about the ceremony was egalitarian—from the fact that the couple walked down the aisle together, to the fact that they each broke a glass, to the fact that the bride's face was not covered with a veil. The bride and groom each took a vow of monogamy, and they wrote up a marriage contract, a legal document listing the main requirements they agreed upon for marriage and explaining how to end the marriage should one or both partners want to do so.

Having the honor of working with this couple on their ceremony and being part of this historic moment was a privilege, and officiating was a pleasure. The ceremony felt completely "Jewish" even without the rings and some of the other traditional elements the couple chose to leave out because of their patriarchal symbolisms. Moreover, nothing was lost without the gender differentiation that is often so highlighted at weddings. The bride and groom are such different people—as are all brides and grooms, all human beings in fact—that there was no need to emphasize her femininity or his masculinity with different gender ritual roles under the chuppah. She did not circle him, and he did not hand her a ring; yet it was clear to everyone present that two unique individuals were coming together to live out their shared dreams, support each other in their individual dreams, help each other grow, and thus do their part in making the world a better place.

Fourth, after a few financial blows, including the general financial crisis of 2008-9, losing our savings in the Madoff scandal, and being robbed three times within four months on Friday night while we were in shul, we decided the time was ripe for a lifestyle change. We felt the need to simplify and get closer to nature. It was time to leave Jerusalem. So we joined a group of families heading north to revive a dying kibbutz members of the Conservative movement had started twenty years before.

The kibbutz, Hannaton, had failed, and the houses were up for sale at a good price. So we rented out our Jerusalem house and headed up north with seventeen other families to revive Kibbutz Hannaton. If we liked it, we decided, we would put our Jerusalem house up for sale later on.

With a mikveh already on site and an education center available for use, my plan was to turn this mikveh into an educational and ritual mikveh, with seminars and other educational programming about mikveh, marriage, and other lifecycle events. Today, "Shmaya: A Ritual and Educational Mikveh" is the only mikveh in Israel run by a woman rabbi and with an open policy of letting anyone who wishes to immerse do so, no questions asked. It is also the only mikveh in Israel where people (gay or straight, single or married, child or adult, Orthodox or liberal Jewish or not even Jewish at all) are encouraged to immerse for both traditional (before a wedding, monthly post-menstruation, before the high holidays, for conversion) and non-traditional rituals (like my miscarriage ritual or other life transitional or healing rituals). When my second daughter, Meira, got her period for the first time, I held her period party in the mikveh, and in addition to the things we did for her sister Michal's party, we added a mikveh immersion ceremony. And, of course, at "Shmaya" men and women are both encouraged to immerse, and couples are encouraged to come to the mikveh together to immerse.

Fifth, one year after all eight of us Ner-Davids settled into life building our liberal Jewish community in the Lower Galilee, I discovered I was pregnant. Nine months later, Shefa-Lee was born. "*Shefa*" means abundance, and "*lee*" means to me. Jacob and I still wonder at the miracle of her existence and count our blessings every day.

Sixth and last, now that we live in the country, we have begun implementing a more basic, more natural, lifestyle. We buy (those we don't grow ourselves or on the kibbutz) mostly organic, locally grown fruits and vegetables, locally produced organic milk products, and locally grown and ground whole wheat flour. We harvest our own olives each year and bring them to be turned into oil at a local olive press, making enough olive oil to last us until the next harvesting season. Adin's summer job (he is now 18 years old!) is working at a local vineyard where Jacob gets the grapes for the Jezreel Winery, that is located at the kibbutz and is his latest startup (in addition to Zula, his new social media start-up). Our eggs come from the five chickens that live in our backyard. And we are in the process of building an environmentally sound house on the kibbutz, complete with a gray water system, solar panels on the roof, and proper natural ventilation and a wood burning fireplace to minimize heating and hopefully prevent having to use air conditioning all together. And, of course, a non-chlorinated naturally filtered (through the use of plants and fish) small lap swimming pool in the side yard for my daily swim.

Another nice result of our move is my development of friendships with local Arabs. Hannaton is surrounded by a variety of Arab villages, and so, naturally, I come in contact with Arab men and women who live in the area on a daily basis. In fact, my current women's group is not a Rosh Chodesh group at all, but rather an Arab-Jewish women's group that meets weekly at various women's houses in the area. I have even begun studying Arabic at the ripe age of 44! And although peace still seems far off, I feel at least in my own life the time of turning inward is over and the time of reaching out has arrived.

Life sends you in unexpected directions. When I was writing this book, I would never have thought seven years later I'd be living on a kibbutz in Galilee with seven children and running the only open, pluralistic, educational mikveh in Israel! But then again, the seeds were all there, waiting for the right time to sprout.

Until the next book...
Rabbi Haviva Ner-David
Kibbutz Mitchadesh Hannaton, 2013

Printed in the USA
CPSIA information can be obtained
at www.ICGtesting.com
LVHW052043020823
753719LV00009B/1226